MODELING AND SIMULATING
COMMUNICATION NETWORKS
A HANDS-ON APPROACH USING
OPNET

Irene Katzela
University of Toronto

PRENTICE HALL, Upper Saddle River, New Jersey 07458

Library of Congress Cataloging-in-Publication Data

Katzela, Irene
 Modeling and simulating communication networks:
 a hands-on approach using OPNET / Irene Katzela.
    p.   cm.
 ISBN   0–13–915737–9
 1. Computer networks–Computer simulation.   2. OPNET   I. Title.
 TK5105.5K37   1999   98–25085
 004.6'01'13–dc21   CIP

Acquisitions Editor: *Tom Robbins*
Production Editor: *Barbara A. Till*
Editor-in-Chief: *Marcia Horton*
Assistant Vice President of Production and Manufacturing: *David W. Riccardi*
Managing Editor: *Eileen Clark*
Manufacturing Buyer: *Donna Sullivan*
Manufacturing Manager: *Trudy Pisciotti*
Creative Director: *Paula Maylahn*
Art Director: *Jayne Conte*
Cover Designer: *Bruce Kenselaar*
Editorial Assistant: *Nancy Garcia*
Copy Editor: *Marjorie Shustak*
Composition: *PreTEX, Inc.*

© 1999 by Prentice-Hall, Inc.
Simon & Schuster / A Viacom Company
Upper Saddle River, New Jersey 07458

For educational use only

The author and publisher of this book have used their best efforts in preparing this book. These efforts include
the development, research, and testing of the theories and programs to determine their effectiveness. The
author and publisher make no warranty of any kind, expressed or implied, with regard to these programs or the
documentation contained in this book. The author and publisher shall not be liable in any event for incidental
or consequential damages in connection with, or arising out of, the furnishing, performance, or use of these
programs.

Printed in the United States of America

10 9 8 7 6 5 4 3 2 1

ISBN 0-13-915737-9

Prentice-Hall International (UK) Limited, *London*
Prentice-Hall of Australia Pty. Limited, *Sydney*
Prentice-Hall Canada Inc., *Toronto*
Prentice-Hall Hispanoamericana, S.A., *Mexico*
Prentice-Hall of India Private Limited, *New Delhi*
Prentice-Hall of Japan, Inc., *Tokyo*
Simon & Schuster Asia Pte. Ltd., *Singapore*
Editora Prentice-Hall do Brasil, Ltda., *Rio de Janeiro*

Contents

Preface

Students of network communications learn about many different network protocols and configurations, but seldom have the opportunity to actively use them and learn first-hand the performance trade-offs involved in designing a network. Network modeling and simulating overcomes this limitation. With it, the students can develop a feel for what is happening in complex network environments by changing parameters and seeing the corresponding impact through performance statistics and animations. It also prepares them to use the modeling tools they will encounter on the job, where new network designs and changes to existing networks must often be proven effective before implementation can proceed.

This book presents six labs that allow students to examine a variety of models for communication systems, protocols, and networks, and the factors that affect their performance.

The first lab, Chapter 2, serves as an introduction to network simulation. It contains a step-by-step example that shows how to use OPNET to construct, execute, and analyze models for communication systems, protocols, and networks. It helps new users familiarize themselves with the OPNET system and user interface. In addition, the example can serve as a representative sequence of modeling activities for evaluating the system against user requirements.

In the second lab, Chapter 3, we provide a set of experiments that study the design and performance of the data link layer protocols. The students examine, via simulation, the behavior of the best-known Automatic Repeat Request (ARQ) protocols, *Stop-and-Wait*, *Go-Back-N*, and *Selective-Repeat*. By varying the simulation parameters the students are able to characterize the performance of ARQ protocols, and compare the schemes under various conditions.

Chapter 4 provides experiments that study several multiaccess protocols. The students examine the performance of Pure Aloha, CSMA, 1-persistent CSMA-CD, and Token Passing Ring Protocols. They study the throughput and delay characteristics of each of the multiaccess protocols and compare their performance under various network conditions.

In the fifth lab, Chapter 5, the students use a set of simulation experiments that studies the performance of a Wide Area Network that provides Frame Relay services to a number of end users. Throughput and end-to-end delay performance of the Frame relay is studied under light, medium, and heavy traffic load conditions.

Chapter 6 addresses performance issues of the Fiber Distributed Data Interface (FDDI) network in a ring topology. Students access, via simulation, the performance of FDDI. Throughput, link utilization and delay issues are studied as a function of design parameters of the FDDI network, like length of the link, number of stations attached to the ring, etc.

Finally, Chapter 7 examines the characteristics of different *Job Service Disciplines*. The student could examine the First-in-First-Out, Priority Job Service. Preempt and Resume, Processor Sharing, Shortest First job service disciplines. The metrics of interest are throughput, delay, variation of delay, average number of customers in the system queue, and fairness they provide to service requests.

This book can be used alone or in conjunction with a text on network communications. The material covered in the book are suitable for an undergraduate course in telecommunication networks (preferably a 4th year course). Each chapter is self-contained, to give the flexibility to the instructor of a first course in telecommunication networks to choose, if preferred only a subset of the provided labs without losing continuity.

The modeling exercises in this lab book are performed with MIL 3's OPNET Modeler, a leading tool for modeling and simulating communications networks. OPNET provides a comprehensive development environment with integrated tools for model design, simulation, data collection, and data analysis. OPNET's detailed protocol models, extensive library of application and vendor-specific device models, and ability to import traffic and topology information make studies of new and existing networks easy.

The authors would like to hear from you about this lab book, including feedback on and corrections to the labs. You can e-mail your comments to university@mil3.com. For further information about OPNET, visit the MIL 3 web site at www.mil3.com.

Qualifications for Software License:

- A school must adopt the lab manual and place a purchase order with Prentice Hall for a minimum of 20 copies.

- A school is required to execute MIL 3, Inc.'s OPNET License and Usage agreement for the Site before a software license and installation is granted.

- The site shall be required to meet the UNIX system requirements as defined on MIL 3, Inc.'s home page (www.mil3.com).

IK

University of Toronto

Chapter 1

Introduction to OPNET

1.1 INTRODUCTION

OPtimized Network Engineering Tools (OPNET) is a comprehensive engineering system capable of simulating large communications networks with detailed protocol modeling and performance analysis. OPNET features include graphical specification of models; a dynamic, event-scheduled Simulation Kernel; integrated data analysis tools; and hierarchical, object-based modeling. OPNET's hierarchical modeling structure accommodates special problems such as distributed algorithm development.

OPNET analyzes system behavior and performance by *discrete-event simulations*, which model system behavior around objects and distinct events such as the arrival of packets at various points in a network. Each object has associated attributes that control its behavior in the simulation. Discrete-event simulation is an approach that supports realistic modeling of complex systems that can be represented as a progression of related events.

OPNET supports modeling efforts with a system of interrelated programs, model libraries, and data files. The primary tool of this system is the **opnet** program, the key features of which include object orientation, graphical specification, automated model creation, an extensive model suite, integrated analysis tools, and animation support. OPNET delivers an open systems methodology and an advanced graphical user interface for building, simulating, and analyzing network models.

This chapter introduces you to **opnet** and explains how to get started using the program. It teaches the fundamentals of using the MIL 3 User Interface (M3UI) and provides a quick overview of the tools available within the **opnet** program. The information provided here concentrates on what you must know to perform the labs in this book. For complete information about OPNET, refer to the online documentation provided on the accompanying CD-ROM.

1.2 RUNNING OPNET

The **opnet** program is the primary application in the OPNET system. It is a window-based application that uses the MIL 3 User Interface (M3UI). M3UI is a graphical user interface (GUI) similar to those used by other interactive applications. M3UI uses windows, dialog boxes, buttons, and scroll bars, and emphasizes mouse input whenever possible.

1.2.1   Invoking OPNET

When the OPNET system software is installed and you have a user account, you are ready to run **opnet**.

TRY IT ... *Invoke opnet*

1. Log into a workstation or remote host that has **opnet** installed.

2. Bring up the window system. (Windows NT, DEC, Silicon Graphics, and HP hosts do this automatically. On Sun hosts, you may have to do it manually.)

3. Create a shell window. (This is usually done automatically by the window system configuration file.)

4. Invoke the **opnet** program by entering the following command:

   opnet

   → The **opnet** window opens.

   The **opnet** screen is divided into multiple areas for different functions. You will learn about these areas in the next section. Within the main workspace of the window, M3UI manages windows for each open *tool*. Tools are "sub-applications" of **opnet**.
   Note: Do not confuse M3UI's internal windows (also called *tool windows*) with the windows managed by the workstation's window system. Tool windows operate by M3UI rules.

1.2.2   Exiting OPNET

The left side of **opnet**'s window has a column of icons called *buttons*. The top group of buttons open various **opnet** tools. The last button of this group exits the program.

TRY IT ... *Exit opnet*

1. Left-click the **Exit opnet** tool button.

   → The **opnet** window closes, and you are returned to the shell window.

   If there is an open tool window with unsaved changes when you try to exit **opnet**, the program displays a confirmation dialog box. Click **OK** to confirm the exit operation or **Cancel** to remain in **opnet**.

1.3   TOOL ENVIRONMENT

The area within an M3UI-based program window is called the *tool environment*. The primary components of this environment are *tool windows* and *button panels*. All of the work related to a particular tool is performed within its tool window. Button panels contain buttons that activate various operations. A tool—also referred to as an *editor*—acts as a subapplication of the program and focuses on a particular modeling aspect.

TRY IT *. . . Invoke opnet*

1. Invoke the **opnet** program before continuing.

The **opnet** program contains the following tools:

- Network Editor—For creating network models.

- Node Editor—For creating node models.

- Process Editor—For creating process models.

- Packet Format Editor—For defining packet formats.

- Parameter Editor—For defining complex parameter values such as probability density functions (PDFs).

- Probe Editor—For specifying what simulation output data should be collected.

- Simulation Tool—For executing simulations.

- Analysis Tool—For analyzing simulation results.

- Filter Tool—For defining mathematical processes for use in the Analysis Tool.

Screen Layout

You can activate the **opnet** tools from the *tool button panel* on the left side of the screen. Multiple tools (including multiple instances of the same tool) can be open at the same time, but only one tool can be used at a time. When a tool is opened, its tool window appears in the large blank area of the screen called the *workspace*. Some of the components, such as tool windows and action buttons, are visible only after you activate a tool from the tool button panel.

The following list briefly describes the various components of the **opnet** screen. The numbers correspond to the callouts in Figure 1.1.

1. Tool button panel—Contains buttons for opening **opnet**'s tools and for exiting **opnet**.

2. Workspace—The area in which tool windows appear. Tool windows cannot extend outside of this area.

3. Action button panel—Contains buttons that are used only with the active tool. These buttons change as different tools become active.

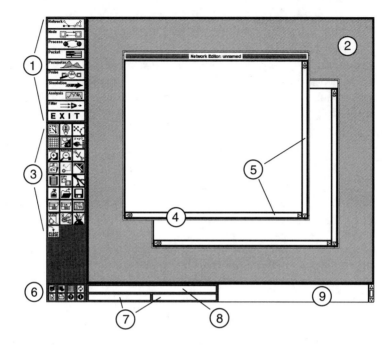

Figure 1.1. Screen Layout.

4. Tool windows—Provide a scrollable view of a tool's model diagram. Multiple tool windows may appear in the workspace at one time. They can be adjacent, overlapping, or stacked.

5. Scroll bars—Tool windows have vertical and horizontal scroll bars used for panning through large diagrams that extend beyond the borders of the tool window. The scroll bars support both slow and fast scrolling.

6. System button panel—Contains buttons for system-level functions such as refreshing the screen, printing, and updating **opnet**'s knowledge of the file system.

7. Mouse switch displays—Indicate the effect of pressing the corresponding left or right mouse switch. The contents of the mouse switch displays change according to where the cursor is positioned and what actions are being performed.

8. Guidance display—Provides hints about button definitions and actions that are pending. The guidance display is especially useful for beginners. Moving the cursor over a panel button displays a message about its function.

9. Message display—Shows status and error messages, with a scroll bar for reviewing previous messages.

1.3.1   Working with Tool Windows

Each time you activate a tool button, a tool window appears in the workspace and the tool's action buttons appear in the action button panel. Most modeling operations (such as creating, viewing, and editing) occur in tool windows. Tool windows can be resized and moved within the confines of the workspace.

Opening a Tool Window

As shown in Figure 1.1, tool buttons are located in the upper left portion of the **opnet** window. To open a tool window in the workspace, left-click the button for the tool you wish to open.

TRY IT   ... *Open a full-size tool window*

1. Move the cursor over the **Open Network Editor** tool button and click the left mouse switch.

→ The Network Editor tool window pops up to occupy the entire workspace area. Notice that a set of smaller buttons appears below the **Exit opnet** button. These are the action buttons for the Network Editor. Each tool has a different set of action buttons.

The header bar of a tool window indicates whether it is active (available for use) or inactive. On color displays, the active tool window has green lines in the header bar, while all other tools have red header bar lines. On monochrome displays, the active tool has black lines; inactive tools have no lines.

To activate an inactive tool window, move the cursor inside the tool window and press the left mouse switch. If inactive windows are hidden, you can bring them forward with the **Circulate Tool Windows** system button.

Resizing Tool Windows

There are two ways to resize a tool window. The fastest method is to double-click on the window's header bar to either increase the window to full size or decrease it to its previous size. Alternatively, you can make a custom-sized window by clicking and dragging the edge of the tool window to a new size.

TRY IT   ... *Open and resize a tool window using the header bar*

1. Move the cursor over the **Open Probe Editor** tool button and click the left mouse switch.

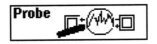

→ The Probe Editor tool window opens and becomes the active window. This window opens slightly smaller than full size, to allow the existing window to be seen.

2. Move the cursor inside the Probe Editor header bar.

→ The cursor changes into four small arrows.

3. Double-click the left mouse switch.

→ The Probe Editor window now fills the entire screen, covering the Network Editor window.

TRY IT   ... *Resize the Probe Editor window by hand*

1. Move the cursor over the right side of the Probe Editor window until the cursor changes into a resize icon (a small arrow and bar).

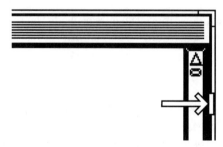

2. Press and hold the left mouse switch.

3. Drag the side or corner of the window until some of the Network Editor becomes visible, then release the mouse switch.

→ The Probe Editor window is redrawn to the new size and the Network Editor window becomes partly visible.

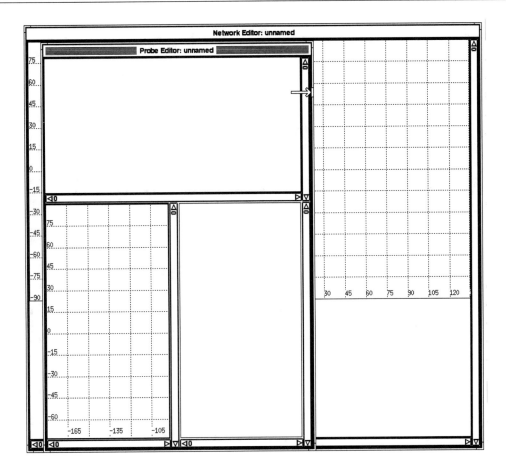

Moving Tool Windows

Moving a tool window is another way to access hidden windows or to make space available for editing or viewing. This "click and drag" technique also works for dialog boxes and other objects in the workspace.

TRY IT ...*Move the Probe Editor window*

1. Move the cursor inside the Probe Editor header bar.

   → The cursor changes into four small arrows.

2. Press and hold the left mouse switch.

   → The Probe Editor window becomes active.

3. Drag the window to a new location within the workspace, then release the mouse switch.

   → The window is redrawn in the new location.

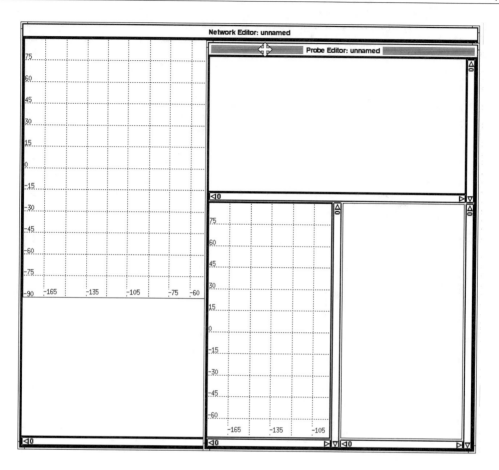

Closing a Tool

Each tool has a **Close** button in its action button area. This button is always in the bottom row of the action button panel.

    Note: Do not press the **Exit** button in the tool button panel to close a tool. This button exits the **opnet** program entirely.

TRY IT   ... *Close the Probe Editor*

1. With the Probe Editor active, move the cursor over the **Exit Probe Editor** action button in the action button panel and click the left mouse switch.

    → The tool window and its action buttons disappear.

1.3.2 Working with Buttons

A *button panel* is an area within the tool environment containing a set of related buttons. (The three button panels—tool, action, and system—were summarized earlier in this chapter.) A button is a small rectangular region used to invoke operations such as opening a tool window, operating on a model, or making a selection from a dialog box.

Invoking an Operation

In OPNET, buttons must be *activated* (selected) before the operation they invoke can be carried out. You activate a button by placing the cursor over it and clicking the left mouse switch.

TRY IT ... *Activate the Set Grid Properties button*

1. Move the cursor over the **Set Grid Properties** button in the Network Editor action button panel.

→ The name of the operation appears in the guidance display.

2. Click the left mouse switch.

→ The operation is invoked. The button is highlighted while its operation is in progress (except tool buttons). In this example, activating the **Set Grid Properties** button causes the Map Grid Properties dialog box to open.

Canceling an Operation

Many operations begin by opening a dialog box. You can cancel these operations by activating the **Cancel** button in the dialog box.

TRY IT ... *Cancel the Set Grid Properties operation*

1. Move the cursor over the **Close** button in the Map Grid Properties dialog box.

2. Click the left mouse switch.

→ The Map Grid Properties dialog box closes, and the Set Grid Properties operation is canceled.

If you begin to activate a button by mistake, you can cancel the operation by moving the cursor away from the button before releasing the mouse switch.

TRY IT ... *Cancel a button activation*

1. Move the cursor over the **Set Grid Properties** button again.

→ The name of the operation appears in the guidance display.

2. Press and hold the left mouse switch.

    → The button is highlighted, but the operation is not yet performed. `Execute operation` appears in the left mouse display, indicating that the operation will be performed when the mouse switch is released.

3. With the left mouse switch still pressed, drag the cursor off the button.

    → `Cancel operation` appears in the left mouse switch display, indicating that the operation will be canceled when the mouse switch is released.

4. Release the left mouse switch.

    → The operation is canceled, and the button is no longer highlighted.

1.4 SYSTEM BUTTONS

The **opnet** system buttons, located in the lower left corner of the **opnet** window, are used to perform system-level operations. These operations are available whether or not a tool is open.

The system buttons are shown in Figure 1.2 and are described in the following list.

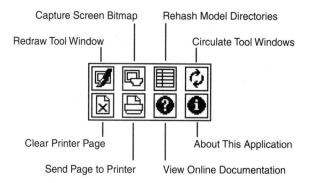

Figure 1.2. System Button Panel.

- Capture Screen Bitmap—Captures and saves (or prints) a graphics bitmap of any part of the program window.

- Redraw Tool Window—Redraws the workspace display.

- Clear Printer Page—Clears the printer page without printing.

- Send Page to Printer—Spools the printer page to the printer, then saves and clears it.

- Rehash Model Directories—Updates the program's internal list of available files.

- Circulate Tool Windows—Brings the bottom-most window to the front and makes it active.

- About This Application—Provides information about the program, the workstation environment, and MIL 3 technical support.

- View Online Documentation—Starts **Acrobat Reader** and displays a menu for selecting the manual to view.

TRY IT   ... *Use a system button*

1. Move the cursor over the **View Online Documentation** system button and click the left mouse switch.

2. When **Acrobat Reader** finishes loading and the initial menu appears, left-click the Modeler document set icon.

   → The Modeler Manual Menu opens.

   You can access any of the manuals in the Modeler documentation set from this screen. For now, use one of **Acrobat Reader**'s most powerful features, the global search function, to find some useful information.

3. Invoke **Acrobat Reader**'s global search function:

   - Left-click the global search button.

   - In the Find Results Containing Text dialog box, type "acrobat."
   - Left-click the **Search** button.
     → The Search Results dialog box opens with a list of every chapter where the word "acrobat" appears.
   - Left-click **System Operations** in the list, then click the **View** button.
     → **Acrobat Reader** opens the *System Operations* chapter to the first instance of the word "acrobat." This section of the *System Operations* chapter contains a short introduction to using **Acrobat Reader**.

4. Close **Acrobat Reader** when you are finished.

1.5   TOOLS

The **opnet** tools fit into three categories, as follows:

Model Development	Simulation Execution	Results Analysis
Network Editor	Probe Editor	Analysis Tool
Node Editor	Simulation Tool	Filter Editor
Process Editor		
Packet Format Editor		
Parameter Editor		

Model Development The primary model development tools are the Network, Node, and Process Editors. Each has the single purpose of defining models at one level of the modeling hierarchy. Typically, initial design efforts in a project will focus on developing node models for each distinct type of node. Process models initially will be placeholders, but will be successively refined during model development. The network model, consisting of nodes and links, must be defined before the network simulation can be built.

The Packet Format Editor is used to define the fields within formatted packets, including field names, types, and sizes.

The Parameter Editor is used during process and node model development to define special model structures such as interface control information (ICI) formats, probability density functions, link models, modulation functions, and antenna patterns.

Simulation Execution Simulation execution typically involves the preparatory step of using the Probe Editor to attach probes to points of interest in a model. The probes record statistics computed during a simulation. The Simulation Tool lets you create simulation sequences that define input and output options for a simulation. This tool also controls execution of a simulation.

Results Analysis For results analysis, you use the Analysis Tool to display statistics gathered during simulations as two-dimensional graphs or text listings. The information collected by a simulation can be viewed directly or processed by filters. The Filter Editor lets you define filters to mathematically process, reduce, or combine statistical data.

The following sections present an overview of the tools you will use in these labs. As you read about each tool, open it and experiment with the various operations available. Then close the tool and continue to the next one. You will learn more about the use of these tools during the labs.

1.5.1 Network Editor

The Network Editor is used to construct network models. Depending on the type of network being modeled, a network model may consist of subnetworks and nodes connected by point-to-point, bus, or radio links. Subnetworks, nodes, and links can be placed within subnetworks, which can then be treated as single objects in the network model. This is useful for separating the network diagram into manageable pieces and provides a quick way of duplicating groups of nodes and links.

Figure 1.3 shows the Network Editor action buttons. Some of these buttons are unique to the Network Editor, while others invoke common operations supported by most tools.

In the following exercises, you will explore the Network Editor and learn how to perform basic operations such as loading, modifying, and saving models.

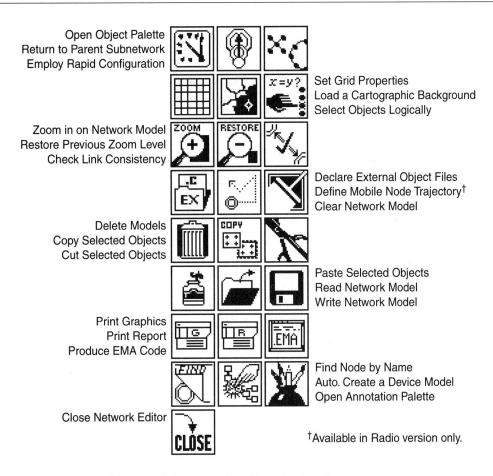

Open Object Palette
Return to Parent Subnetwork
Employ Rapid Configuration

Set Grid Properties
Load a Cartographic Background
Select Objects Logically

Zoom in on Network Model
Restore Previous Zoom Level
Check Link Consistency

Declare External Object Files
Define Mobile Node Trajectory†
Clear Network Model

Delete Models
Copy Selected Objects
Cut Selected Objects

Paste Selected Objects
Read Network Model
Write Network Model

Print Graphics
Print Report
Produce EMA Code

Find Node by Name
Auto. Create a Device Model
Open Annotation Palette

Close Network Editor

†Available in Radio version only.

Figure 1.3. Network Editor Action Buttons.

Working with Model Files

Network models are stored in separate files on disk (as are all models created with **opnet** tools). To view or edit a model, you must read the model file into the appropriate tool. The tool then stores the model in a buffer. Changes made to a model affect only the copy held in the buffer. To make changes permanent, you must write the model back to disk. Figure 1.4 illustrates this process.

Each tool has **Read Model** and **Write Model** buttons in its action button panel. (For the purpose of these buttons, *model* is a generic term representing any type of file created by a tool, such as network models, probe files, and simulation sequences. Thus, the exact names of these buttons vary between tools.) In the Network Editor, you use these buttons to load and save network models.

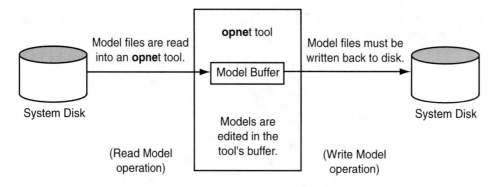

Figure 1.4. Working with Model Files.

Model Directories

Any directory used to store model files is called a *model directory*. OPNET comes with a variety of model directories holding different types of predefined models. The **opnet** program knows where to look for model files by examining a list of directories specified in the environment database file (<*HOME*>/op_admin/env_db40) by the **mod_dirs** environment attribute. The first directory listed is called the primary model directory; all new network models you create will be placed there when saved. By default, the primary model directory is <*HOME*>/op_models. To save new models in a different directory, edit the list of directories in the **mod_dirs** environment attribute to put the desired directory first.

The standard models supplied with OPNET include a predefined network model called **eth-coax_net**. You will work with this model in the following exercises, so let's begin by loading it into the Network Editor.

TRY IT ... *Read a model from disk*

1. Left-click the **Read Network Model** action button in the Network Editor action button panel.

   → A dialog box pops up with a list of available files.

2. Left-click **ethcoax_net** in the file list.

   → The model is read into the tool window. You may need to resize the Network Editor window to view the entire model.

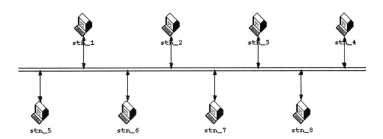

While there is a model in the Network Editor window, let's look at how you can modify it. **opnet** lets you select, cut, copy, paste, and move objects in a tool window. You will often use these operations to duplicate objects in a model or rearrange a model to make it more legible.

Selecting Objects

You can select any object in a tool window by left-clicking it. You must select objects before performing many types of operations on them, such as cutting, copying, and certain kinds of editing.

TRY IT . . . *Select an object*

1. Move the cursor over the **stn_1** icon and left-click the mouse.

   → Selection markers appear around the icon.

Objects remain selected until you deselect them. To deselect an object, left-click it.

TRY IT . . . *Deselect an object*

1. Move the cursor over the **stn_1** icon and left-click the mouse.

   → The selection markers disappear from the icon.

You can select multiple objects by left-clicking each in turn. However, you can also select a group of objects by dragging a selection rectangle around them. All objects completely enclosed by the rectangle will be selected.

TRY IT   . . . *Select a group of objects*

1. Move the cursor to a point above and to the left of the **stn_1** icon.

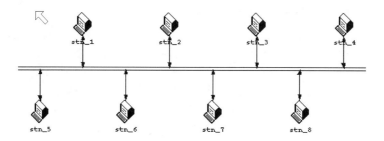

2. While pressing the left mouse switch, drag the cursor until it is below the bus and to the right of the **stn_4** icon.

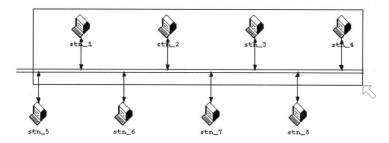

→ As the cursor moves, a rubber-band selection rectangle tracks its movement.

3. Release the mouse switch.

   → Selection markers appear on all objects entirely enclosed by the selection rectangle.

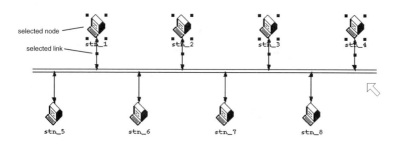

opnet also provides a way to quickly deselect all objects.

TRY IT   ...*Deselect all objects*

1. Move the cursor to an empty part of the tool window and left-click the mouse.

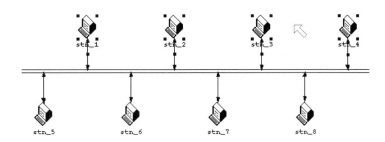

    → The selection markers disappear from all objects.

Moving Objects

You can move objects in a tool window by dragging them to the desired location. If the objects being moved are connected to other objects by links, the links remain attached throughout the move.

TRY IT   ...*Move a node*

1. Move the cursor over **stn_1**.

2. Press and hold the left mouse switch while moving the mouse until the node outline is positioned below the bus.

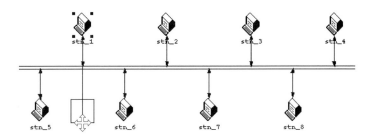

3. Release the mouse switch.

    → The node icon moves to the location indicated by its outline, and the outline disappears. Notice that **stn_1** is now selected.

If several objects are selected, they will all move together.

TRY IT ... *Move several nodes*

1. Left-click the **stn_1** icon to deselect it.

2. Click and drag across **stn_2**, **stn_3**, and **stn_4** to select them.

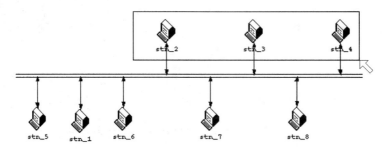

3. Move the cursor over any selected node.

4. Press and hold the left mouse switch while moving the mouse until the node outlines are positioned below the bus.

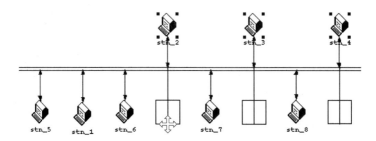

→ The node outlines move together, maintaining their positions relative to each other.

5. Release the mouse switch.

→ The node icons move to the locations indicated by their outlines, and the outlines disappear. All three nodes remain selected.

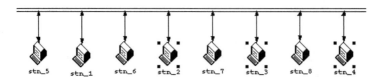

Saving Models

Because you have changed the network model, you must save it before exiting the Network Editor or your changes will be lost. If you try to exit a tool without saving changes, the **opnet** program will remind you to do so.

TRY IT ... *Write a model to disk*

1. Left-click the **Write Network Model** action button.

2. Type "my_ethcoax_net" in the highlighted area. Note that the mouse cursor does not have to be inside the dialog box in order for you to type.

   Model names can include letters, digits, underscores, and hyphens. The maximum length is 48 characters.

3. Left-click **OK**.

   → The dialog box closes and the file is saved. Because this is a new model, it is saved in your primary model directory. Existing files are saved in their original directories.

Most dialog boxes have a default button, which is indicated by a double outline (such as **OK** in the Enter Value dialog box). You can activate the default button by left-clicking it, as usual, or by pressing the <Return> key.

If you try to write a file using a name that already exists, **opnet** displays a confirmation dialog box. When this happens, left-click **OK** to confirm the write operation or **Cancel** to not write the file.

You will come back to the Network Editor in your first lab. For now, close the Network Editor and move on to the Node Editor.

TRY IT ... *Exit the Network Editor*

1. Left-click the **Exit Network Editor** action button.

   → The Network Editor closes, and its action buttons disappear.

1.5.2 Node Editor

The Node Editor is used to create models of nodes. The node models are then used to create node instances within networks in the Network Editor. Internally, OPNET node models have a modular structure. You define a node by connecting various modules with packet streams and statistic wires. The connections between modules allow packets and status information to be exchanged between modules. Each module placed in a node serves a specific purpose, such as generating packets, queuing packets, processing packets, or transmitting and receiving packets.

Figure 1.5 shows the Node Editor action buttons. Some of these buttons (such as **Create Ideal Generator**) are unique to the Node Editor; others (such as **Copy Selected Objects**) are general operations supported by most tools.

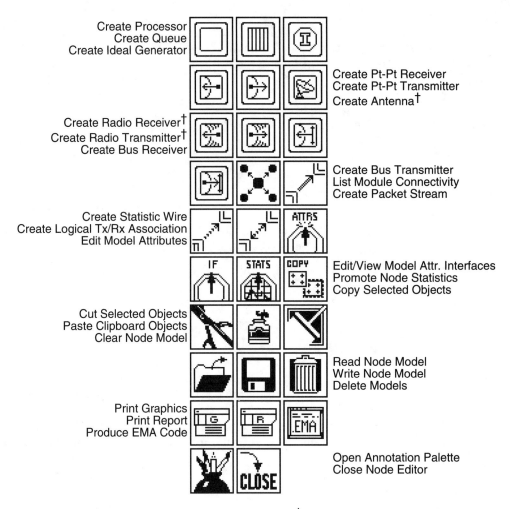

Create Processor
Create Queue
Create Ideal Generator

Create Pt-Pt Receiver
Create Pt-Pt Transmitter
Create Antenna[†]

Create Radio Receiver[†]
Create Radio Transmitter[†]
Create Bus Receiver

Create Bus Transmitter
List Module Connectivity
Create Packet Stream

Create Statistic Wire
Create Logical Tx/Rx Association
Edit Model Attributes

Edit/View Model Attr. Interfaces
Promote Node Statistics
Copy Selected Objects

Cut Selected Objects
Paste Clipboard Objects
Clear Node Model

Read Node Model
Write Node Model
Delete Models

Print Graphics
Print Report
Produce EMA Code

Open Annotation Palette
Close Node Editor

[†] Available in Radio version only

Figure 1.5. Node Editor Action Buttons.

Loading Node Models

TRY IT   *. . . Read a node model*

1. Open the Node Editor by left-clicking the **Open Node Editor** tool button.

2. Activate the **Read Model** button in the Node Editor action button panel.

   → A dialog box pops up with a list of available files.

3. Select **ethcoax_station_base** in the file list.

   → The model is read into the tool window.

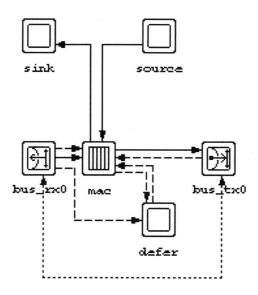

Viewing Node Attributes

In **opnet**, objects are described by attributes. You can view and edit the attribute values for an object in its Attributes dialog box. An attribute is defined by a set of properties, including a data type, default value, units, and a comment describing the attribute. There is also a range of values and a symbol map that can constrain the values allowed for the attribute. The properties are also available for you to view.

TRY IT *... View the properties for an attribute*

1. Right-click on the queue module (**mac**).

→ The Attributes dialog box appears. Notice that the process model for this queue module is **eth_mac**.

2. Select the **icon name** attribute by left-clicking it in the Attributes column, then click the **View Properties** button.

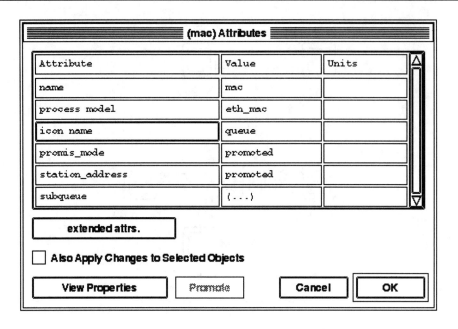

→ A dialog box opens showing the attribute's properties.

3. Review the description and other information.

4. Click **Close** to close the dialog box showing the properties of the **icon name** attribute.

5. Click **Cancel** to close the dialog box showing the **mac** attributes.

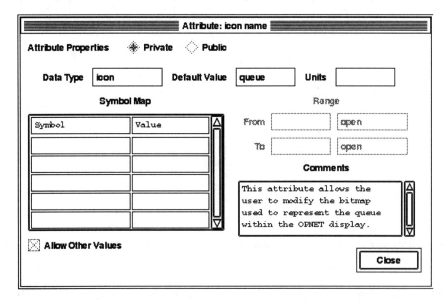

6. Explore some of the operations invoked by other Node Editor action buttons, then exit the Node Editor by clicking the **Close** button in the action button panel.

1.5.3 Probe Editor

The Probe Editor allows you to gain insight into a model's dynamic operation by collecting data through probes. A *probe* represents a request to collect a particular piece of data about a simulation. You can create various types of probes to collect any combination of local or system-wide statistics, attribute values, and animation data.

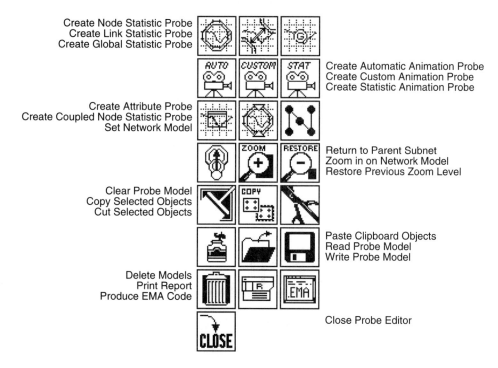

Figure 1.6. Probe Editor Action Buttons.

TRY IT ... *Open the Probe Editor*

1. Activate the **Open Probe Editor** tool button.

→ The Probe Editor tool window and action buttons appear.

The Probe Editor tool window is divided into three areas, as shown in Figure 1.7. Probes are placed in the probe workspace. The lower portion of the Probe Editor window is divided into two subwindows that contain diagrams of the network and node models being probed. These lower subwindows provide a means for selecting particular nodes and modules as probe points.

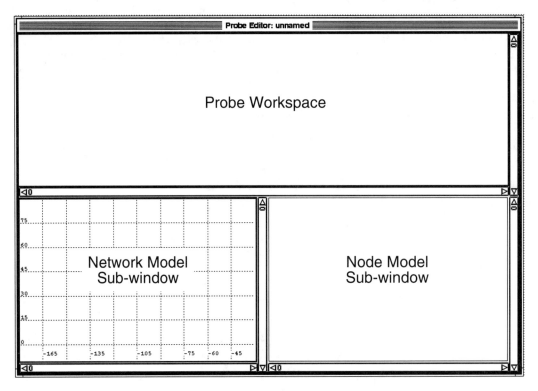

Figure 1.7. Probe Editor Window.

Loading Probes

The Probe Editor lets you define sets of probes that collect information from a model when it is simulated. You can define different sets of probes for the same network model and use them in different simulations, or define one set and modify it as needed. The standard model directories include a probe file for the **ethcoax_net** model you saw in the Network Editor.

TRY IT   ... *Load the probe file*

1. Activate the **Read Probe Model** action button.

   → A dialog box pops up with a list of available files.

2. Left-click **ethcoax_net** in the file list.

   → The probe file is read into the probe workspace.

This probe file contains several different predefined probes. The node statistic probe named **S1 Act Load** collects data on the actual load processed by a single node. The global statistic probe named **Eth Act Load** collects data on the total network load.

Viewing Attributes

Probes (like other **opnet** objects) have associated attributes that define them. These attributes can be viewed and modified in the object's Attributes dialog box. You can use this dialog box to learn more about node statistic probe **S1 Act Load**.

TRY IT ... *View probe attributes*

1. Right-click the **S1 Act Load** probe icon in the probe workspace.
    → The Attributes dialog box opens.

Attribute	Value	Units
name	S1 Act Load	
subnet	ethcoax_net	
node	stn_1	
module		
submodule		
statistic	Ethernet Actual	
ordinate label		
vector data	enabled	

☐ **Also Apply Changes to Selected Objects**

View Properties	Promote	**Cancel**	**OK**

This dialog box lets you view the current attribute values or set new ones. You can specify what data the probe will collect and how it will collect it. You can choose the statistic name and source, whether to collect vector or scalar statistics (or both), time windows for collection, and so on.

Notice that the **S1 Act Load** probe is set to collect the **Ethernet Actual Load (bits/sec)** statistic from **stn_1** of the network. (To see the full name, right-click the **statistic** attribute's value, then left-click when finished.) The data will be collected as vector data, which means that a value will be recorded at each time step of the simulation.

Now close the Probe Editor and move on to the Simulation Tool.

TRY IT   ... *Exit the Probe Editor*

  1. Left-click the **Cancel** button to close the dialog box.

  2. Activate the **Exit Probe Editor** action button.

1.5.4   Simulation Tool

You use the Simulation Tool to graphically set up and execute simulations by creating *simulation set* objects, each of which can represent one or more simulation runs. Simulation sets are defined by selecting the network model to be executed and then specifying values for input parameters such as random number seed, duration, and output file names for probed data. You can also choose to execute the model with a range or series of values for particular attributes. This causes the simulation set object to execute multiple simulation runs, one for each unique set of values. While simulations execute, you can either monitor and control their progress through dialog box buttons or run them in the background while you work in other **opnet** tools.

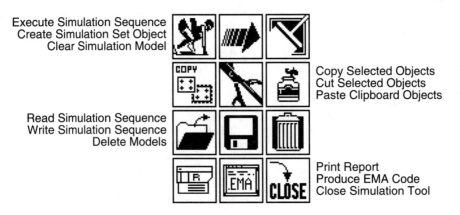

Figure 1.8. Simulation Tool Action Buttons.

TRY IT   ... *Open the Simulation Tool*

  1. Activate the **Open Simulation Tool** tool button.

  → The Simulation Tool action buttons and tool window appear.

Loading Simulation Sequences

Files that define how to run a simulation are called *simulation sequences* and are loaded just like network models and probe files.

TRY IT ... *Load the simulation sequence*

1. Activate the **Read Simulation Sequence** action button.

   → A dialog box pops up with a list of available files.

2. Left-click **ethcoax_net** in the file list.

   → The simulation sequence is read into the tool window. Notice that the simulation is an object and is represented in the workspace by an icon.

Modifying Simulation Sequences

The attributes of a simulation set specify which network and probe files to use, what output files to create, the duration of the simulation, and the values of simulation variables. As with other objects, you can open a dialog box to view or modify the attributes of a simulation set.

TRY IT ... *Set the simulation duration*

1. Right-click the simulation set icon.

   → The Simulation Set dialog box opens.

2. Left-click over the **Duration** text entry area.

3. Change the simulation duration:

   • Drag the cursor across the current value to select it.
   • Type "15" and press <Return>. This value will shorten the simulation run to about
     2 minutes of real time (depending on the speed of your computer).

4. In the same way, change the **Update intvl** value to "5."

5. Press <Return> to activate the default **OK** button.

   → The new values are set and the dialog box closes.

Running Simulation Sequences

Once a simulation is defined, you can run it by clicking a button.

TRY IT   ...*Run the simulation*

1. Activate the **Execute Simulation Sequence** action button.

   → The Simulation Sequence dialog box appears, and the simulation begins executing.

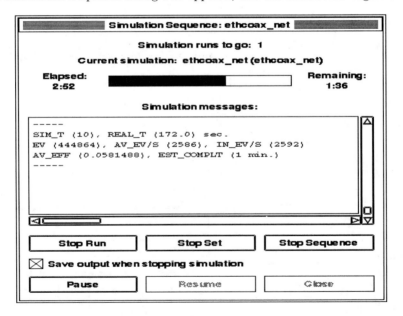

This dialog box reports the progress of the simulation as it is compiled and executed. It
also allows you to control the execution by pausing or stopping the simulation.

2. When the simulation run is finished, left-click **Close**.

> → The Simulation Sequence dialog box closes.

Now that you have simulated the network and collected some data, you can leave the Simulation Tool and analyze the data in the Analysis Tool.

TRY IT   . . . *Exit the Simulation Tool*

1. Activate the **Exit Simulation Tool** action button.

> → A confirmation dialog box appears (because you changed the **Duration** and **Update Intvl** attribute values without saving the simulation sequence).

2. Left-click **OK**.

> → The Simulation Tool closes without saving the changes.

1.5.5   Analysis Tool

You use the Analysis Tool to evaluate the results of a simulation. You can graphically display the statistics collected from a simulation run (or series of runs) in a variety of graph types. You can also apply filters to the graphs to generate new sets of data.

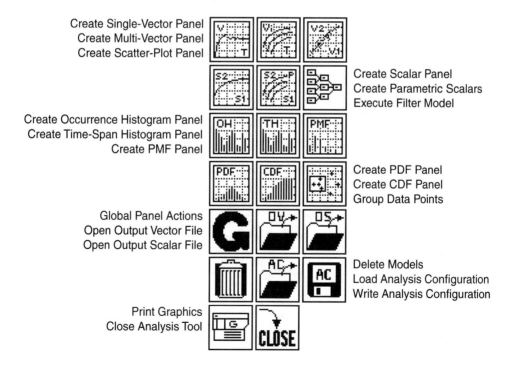

Figure 1.9. Analysis Tool Action Buttons.

TRY IT ... *Open the Analysis Tool*

1. Activate the **Open Analysis Tool** tool button.

→ The Analysis Tool action buttons and tool window appear.

Loading Data Files

All vector data collected during a simulation is saved in a single file. Open the data file created by the simulation you just ran.

TRY IT ... *Load the output vector file*

1. Activate the **Open Output Vector File** action button.

   → A dialog box appears listing the available output vector files.

2. Left-click **ethcoax_net** in the list of vector files.

   → **opnet** opens the selected data file.

   Note: There will be no indication that the file has been opened.

Applying Data to Templates

OPNET allows you to simplify data analysis by creating analysis panels containing *templates*, which are preformatted traces (plots) that do not hold any data. You can save the template panels in *analysis configuration* files and load them as needed. Then, when you apply data to them, it is automatically formatted for display.

TRY IT ... *Load an analysis configuration and apply data to it*

1. Activate the **Load Analysis Configuration** action button.

   → A dialog box appears listing the available analysis configurations.

2. Left-click **ethcoax_net** in the list of analysis configurations.

   → **opnet** opens the selected analysis configuration and displays it in the workspace. Because the displayed analysis panels contain templates and an output vector file is loaded, **opnet** also pops up the Load Configuration dialog box.

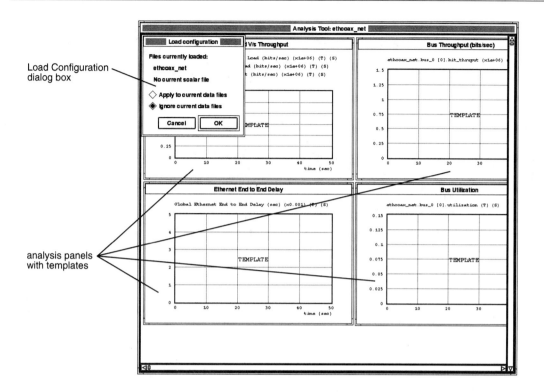

3. Left-click the **Apply to current data files** radio button, then left-click **OK**.

    → **opnet** applies data in the currently loaded files to any matching templates in the workspace. (To match, the data and template must have the same statistic name.)

The panel titled Ethernet Load v/s Throughput (shown in Figure 1.10) contains the data collected by probe **Eth Act Load** (the **Global Ethernet Specified Load (bits/sec)** statistic). The other traces in this panel and those in the remaining panels represent data collected by other probes in the **ethcoax_net** probe file.

When you have finished examining these analysis panels, you can remove them from the workspace to make room for additional analysis.

TRY IT   ... *Delete the analysis panels*

1. Activate the **Global Panel Actions** action button.

    → The Global Actions dialog box appears.

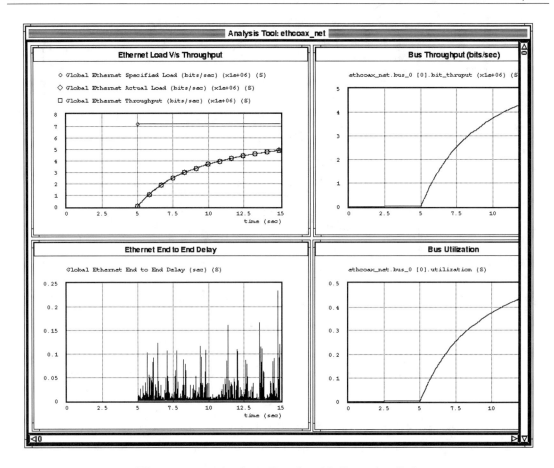

Figure 1.10. Analysis Panels with Data Applied.

2. Make sure the **Remove all panels** radio button is selected, then left-click **OK**.

   → A confirmation dialog box appears.

3. Left-click **OK**.

   → All analysis panels are deleted from the workspace.

Creating an Analysis Panel

OPNET provides a variety of ways in which you can graph simulation data. To see the data collected by the **S1 Act Load** probe (which was not included in the analysis configuration), you can plot a single statistic trace.

TRY IT   . . . *Plot a single vector*

1. Activate the **Create Single-Vector Panel** action button.

→ A dialog box appears with a list of the traces available in the **ethcoax_net** output vector file. These traces are the data collected by the statistic probes you saw in the Probe Editor.

2. Left-click **ethcoax_net.stn_1.Ethernet Actual Load (bits/sec)**.

   → The dialog box closes automatically.

3. Select an area for the analysis panel, as follows:

   - Move the cursor into the tool window near the upper left corner.
   - Press and hold the left mouse switch.
   - Drag the cursor to a location near the center of the tool window.
     → As the cursor moves, a rubber-band rectangle outline tracks its movement. The outline represents the area in which the panel will be created.
   - Release the mouse switch.
     → **opnet** creates the panel in the tool window and draws the selected trace (shown in Figure 1.11).

Modifying an Analysis Panel

You can change many characteristics of an analysis panel by editing its attributes. There are two kinds of dialog boxes associated with analysis panels.

- The Edit Panel dialog box affects panel-wide characteristics such as the panel title, range and label of the abscissa axis, and panel location. You open this dialog box by right-clicking in the border area of an active panel.

- The Edit Zone dialog box affects characteristics of a particular zone (the area in which traces are drawn). You can change the color of traces, the ordinate axis range and label, and the drawing style, among other things. You open this dialog box by right-clicking in the zone you want to alter (the analysis panel must be active).

TRY IT ...*Edit the panel*

1. Left-click in the zone of the open panel.

   → The Edit Zone dialog box opens.

2. Change some of the values, then click the **Apply** button to see the effect on the panel.

3. Click **OK** to close the dialog box.

You have now finished your overview of the OPNET network modeling process. Exit the Analysis Tool and leave the **opnet** program.

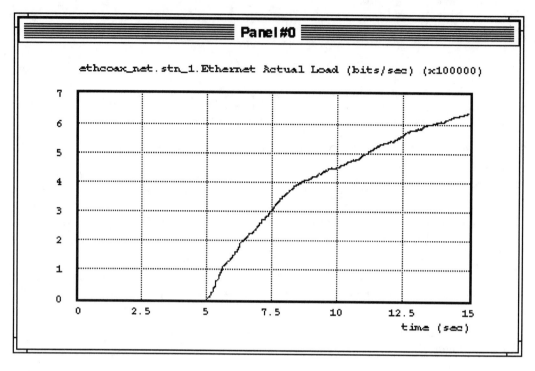

Figure 1.11. Ethernet Actual Load Vector Analysis Panel.

TRY IT ... *Exit the Analysis Tool and OPNET*

1. Activate the **Exit Analysis Tool** action button.

    → A confirmation dialog box appears (because you have not saved the analysis panel).

2. Left-click **OK**.

    → The Analysis Tool closes without saving the analysis panel.

3. Activate the **Exit opnet** tool button.

    → The **opnet** program closes.

1.6   ONLINE DOCUMENTATION

The CD-ROM that accompanies this lab book contains the complete documentation set for
OPNET Modeler, as does the online documentation within an OPNET installation. This documentation is provided in Adobe Acrobat format. If **Acrobat Reader** is installed on your
computer, you can view the online manuals without running **opnet** by opening the following file
on the CD-ROM:

        doc/modeler/Modeler_ManualMenu.pdf

Note: If the text appears blurred on your display, turn off the Smooth Text and Monochrome Images option in the **Acrobat Reader** General Preferences dialog box.

1.6.1   Installing Acrobat Reader

If you need to install **Acrobat Reader** on your computer, run the appropriate installer from the CD-ROM:

Windows NT: `ACROREAD\WINDOWS\SETUP.EXE`

UNIX: `acroread/unix/INSTALL`

1.6.2   Navigating Online Documentation

Acrobat Reader provides a control bar with buttons for moving forward and backward through a file, retracing your path through the documentation, and searching the manual set for specific text. *Bookmarks* along the left side of the **Acrobat Reader** window let you jump directly to corresponding headings in the current file, to the beginning of other files, and to menus. You can also jump through the documentation by clicking headings in a manual's table of contents or entries (page numbers) in any index.

Figure 1.12. Acrobat Reader Control Bar.

The following table describes the navigation buttons that appear on the control bar.

Button	Name	Description
	Full Page	Hides all bookmarks and thumbnails.
	Bookmarks and Page	Displays the bookmarks in the current document.
	Thumbnails and Page	Displays thumbnails in the current document.
	Hand	Selects the hand tool, which can be used to move a page within the window or to follow links. Cursor changes to a pointing finger when positioned over a link.
	Zoom	Selects the zoom tool used to increase or decrease the magnification of the current document.
	Text Selection	Selects the text selection tool. Used to select text for copying.
	First Page	Moves to first page of current file.
	Previous Page	Returns to the previous page in the current file.
	Next Page	Moves ahead to the next page in current file.
	Last Page	Moves to last page of current file.
	Go Back	Returns to the previous page, document, or magnification level.
	Go Forward	Returns, one view at a time, to the view where the Go Back button was first used.
	Default View	Sets the zoom level to 100%.
	Fit Page	Sets the zoom level such that the entire page fits within the main window.
	Fit Width	Sets the zoom level such that the width of the page fits within the main window.
	Find	Searches the currently open file for user-denied keywords.
	Search	Searches the entire manual set, including unopened files, for user-defined keywords.
	Search Results	Shows results of the last search.
	Search Previous	Returns to the previous item view that was returned by a search.
	Search Next	Moves to the next item view that was returned by a search.

Chapter 2

Introduction to Network Simulation: M/M/1 Queue Example

OPNET is a sophisticated workstation-based environment for the modeling and simulation of communication systems, protocols, and networks. This lab serves as a brief introduction to the basic techniques and user interface procedures that an OPNET user requires. OPNET is designed to model a wide variety of computer architectures, from a single processor to a complex system of processors and storage devices connected in a network. Animation and event trace messages describing simulation activity can be displayed. Device status and utilization as function of time can be plotted. End-of-simulation reports are created that can be viewed or printed out as documentation.

2.1 Objectives

This lab contains a step-by-step example that shows how to use OPNET to construct, execute, and analyze models for communications systems, protocols, and networks. It plays a vital role in helping new users familiarize themselves with the OPNET system and user interface. In addition, the example can serve as a representative sequence of modeling activities for evaluating the system against user requirements.

The featured example is an M/M/1 queue design and analysis. It presents a practical example of creating a simulation executable, running simulations, and analyzing simulation results. It also demonstrates particular uses of the **Node Editor**, **Network Editor**, **Probe Editor**, **Simulation Tool**, and **Analysis Tool**. The material presented here are based on the M/M/1 queue tutorial documentation that accompanies the OPNET modeler.

2.2 M/M/1 Queue

An M/M/1 queue consists of a First-In First-Out (FIFO) buffer with packets arriving randomly according to a Poisson arrival process, and a processor, called the server, that retrieves packets from the buffer at a specified service rate. The performance of an M/M/1 queue system depends on three parameters: packet arrival rate, packet sizes, and service capacity.

The task is to construct an M/M/1 queue model and observe the performance of the queuing system as the packet arrival rates, packet sizes, and service capacities change. We will measure three statistics: the average delay, called waiting time, experienced by packets in the queue; the number of packets in the queue at any point in time; and the average number of packets in the queue over time. A variety of queuing systems that use different *service disciplines* will be studied, in detail, in Chapter 7.

2.2.1   Designing the Model

OPNET models are hierarchical. At the lowest level, the behavior of an algorithm or a protocol is encoded by a state/transition diagram, called *state machine*, with embedded code based on *C-type* language constructs. At the middle level, discrete functions such as buffering, processing, transmitting, and receiving data packets are performed by separate *objects*. Some of these objects rely on underlying process models. In OPNET, we call these objects *modules*, and they are created, modified, and edited in the Node Editor within OPNET. Modules are connected to form a higher-level node model. At the highest level, node objects are deployed and connected by links to form a network model. The network model defines the scope of the simulation.

The task is to create a node model that emulates an M/M/1 queue. An M/M/1 queuing system is generally depicted as in Figure 2.1. The parameters λ,$1/\mu$, and C represent the mean packet arrival rate, the mean service requirement (mean packet size), and service (outgoing link) capacity, respectively. The model requires a means for generating, queuing, and servicing data packets. All those capabilities are provided by existing OPNET modules and models.

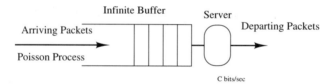

Figure 2.1. M/M/1 Queue.

2.2.2   Entering the Model

The lower-level objects required for an M/M/1 queue are provided by OPNET, but they need to be combined to form a node model. Open the Node Editor by clicking the **Node Editor** tool button.

Create the Node Model

1. Create a **source** module. Define the module that will randomly produce packets. OP-NET provides an ideal generator module that creates packets according to a user-specified probability distribution. To create an ideal generator module:

   - Activate the **Create Ideal Generator** action button. When you move the cursor inside the tool window, it changes and shows the outline of a box. Place the box in the position you like inside the tool window and left-click the mouse. The ideal generator has been created.

- Open the attribute dialog box of the generator by right-clicking the ideal generator's icon.

- Change the attributes of the module as follows:

  - Change the name of the module to **src** (for source). To change an attribute value, click the left button of the mouse in the value column, enter the text, and then press <Return> to ensure that the data is entered.

  - Change the **interarrival pdf** to "exponential." For the M/M/1 queue we require Poisson arrival distribution of the input data stream. To achieve that, the interarrival of packets must be exponentially distributed.

  - Promote the **interarrival args** attribute to the simulation level by moving the cursor over the attribute and pressing the *middle* mouse switch, or by selecting the **interarrival args** attribute and left-clicking the **Promote** button. The **interarrival args** attribute defines the mean interarrival rate of the packet. Since this is one of the parameters that define the behavior of the queue, we would like to vary it. In order to do so, we will "promote" the value of this attribute to the network level. Promoting an attribute allows its value to be specified during simulation time.

  - Set the **pk size pdf** to "exponential." This sets the size of the generated packets to be exponentially distributed.

  - Promote the service requirements by promoting the **pk size args** attribute.

- Close the dialog box by clicking the **OK** button.

Now the ideal generator's definition for the source (**src**) is complete. During simulation, **src** will randomly generate packets according to the **interarrival pdf** values assigned.

2. Create a **queue** module.

   - Activate the **Create Queue** action button and place a queue model to the right of the ideal generator model inside the tool window.

   - Open the attribute dialog box of the queue by right-clicking the queue icon.

   - Change the name attribute to **FIFO_queue**.

   - Change the process model to **acb_fifo**. The **acb_fifo** process is an OPNET-supplied process model that provides service in the packets arriving in the queue according to FIFO discipline. Note that when a process model is assigned to a module, the process model attributes appear in the module's attribute menu. The **acb_fifo** model has an attribute called **service_rate**. When you select the **acb_fifo** process model, the **service_rate** attribute appears in the queue module's attribute menu with the default value 9600 bits per second.

   - Promote the attribute for **service_rate** to the higher level. To do so, click the left mouse button on the values field of the service rate attribute and then click the promote button. The **service_rate** attribute represents the service capacity of the queue process model's built-in server.

   - Close the dialog box by clicking the **OK** button.

3. Create a **sink** module. For proper memory management, packets should be destroyed when no longer needed. The OPNET-supplied sink process model destroys packets sent to it. To create the sink module:

- Activate the **Create Processor** action button and place a processor to the right of the queue model in the tool window. Don't forget to right-click the mouse to end the placement of an object in the tool window.
- Open the attribute box for the processor module by right-clicking the icon. Notice that the default value for the process model attribute is **sink**.
- Close the dialog box by clicking the **OK** button.

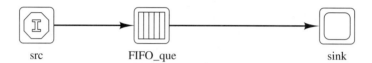

src   FIFO_que   sink

Figure 2.2. M/M/1 Node.

4. Connect the modules with packet streams. Packet streams provide a path for the transfer of packets between modules. They serve as one-way paths and are depicted by solid arrowed lines.

- Activate the **Create Packet Stream** action button.
- Connect the **src** module with the queue module by clicking the **src** icon, then clicking the queue icon. Remember that the first module you click becomes the source, and the second one the destination.
- Connect the queue module and the sink module. Remember to end the **Create Packet Stream** operation by right-clicking anywhere in the window.
- Open the attribute dialog box of a packet stream by clicking the right mouse button on either arrow. Notice that the default value of the **dest_stream** is "0." OPNET automatically chooses connection ports.
- Close the dialog box by clicking the **OK** button. The complete node model is depicted in Figure 2.2.

5. Save the model by activating the **Write Node Model** action button. Name the file **mm1_node** and press <Return>.

6. Activate the **Exit Node Editor** action button.

The M/M/1 node model definition is complete. The node model will be referenced by a node object at the network level.

Create the Network Model

Now we are ready to create the network model. The M/M/1 network model will consist of a single node object based on the **mm1_node** model. The Network Editor is used to define the network model and create the simulation executable.

1. Open the Network Editor by clicking the **Network Editor** tool button.

2. Create a fixed communication node as follows:

   - Activate the **Open Object Palette** action button. The object palette dialog box appears.
   - Enable the **Model List** radio button and then select the **mm1_palette** from the list of possible palettes. The **mm1_palette** has been created for you and contains only the objects you need to create the M/M/1 queue single node network.

   In the Palette, click the **mm1_node** communication node and continue to hold the mouse button down. Place the cursor inside the tool window. The cursor changes and shows the outline box. Drag the box into the tool window. When the box is where you want the node icon to be, release the mouse button. The icon appears in the tool window. Right-click to end the operation.

   - Change the attributes of the node.
     - Open the attribute dialog box of the node by right-clicking the icon.
     - Change the value of the **name** attribute to **mm1**. Notice that the model attribute is **mm1_node**.
     - Close the dialog box by clicking the **OK** button.

3. Write the Network Model by activating the **Write Network Model** action button. Name the file **mm1_net**.

4. Exit the Network Editor.

Now the M/M/1 queue model is completely defined.

2.2.3 Specifying Probes

As we mentioned in the introduction, a number of statistics will be monitored during simulation. These must be selected using the **Probe Editor**. Specifying appropriate probes causes the statistics to be recorded at simulation time.

1. Open the Probe Editor by clicking the **Probe Editor** tool button.

2. Activate the **Set Network Model** action button.

3. Select **mm1_net** from the menu of available files. This displays the network diagram in the network subwindow.

4. Activate the **Create Node Statistic Probe** action button and place a probe anywhere in the probe area window.

5. Use the selection method to change the attributes of the probe as follows:

   - Click the probe icon to select it. Four corner markers appear around the icon.

- Click the **mm1_node** in the network subwindow. This adds the subnet and node information to the probe's attributes and displays the node model diagram in the node subwindow.

- Click the queue module in the node diagram. The probe's attribute dialog box now specifies **queue** as the module to be probed.

- Change the submodule attribute to subqueue [0].

- Change the statistic attribute to "mean_delay."

- Close the dialog box by clicking the **OK** button.

- Deselect **pb0** by clicking in a blank portion of the tool window.

- Specify the remaining statistic probes **pb1** and **pb2**. Before selecting a new probe, be sure to deselect the previous probe to avoid multiple selected probes. The **pb1** statistic probe records the **pksize**, and **pb2** the **mean pksize**. Specify them by following similar steps as above and change the statistic attribute to **pksize** for **pb1**, and **mean pksize** for **pb2**. The **mean delay** probe keeps track of the average delay that packets experience in the queue. The **pksize** probe records the instantaneous number of packets in the queue at all simulation times. The **mean pksize** probe records the average number of packets in the queue during the simulation.

6. Close the dialog box by clicking the **OK** button.

7. Activate the **Write Probe Model** action button. Name the file **mm1_probe** and press \<Return\>.

8. Activate the **Exit Probe Editor** action button.

2.2.4   Executing the Simulation

The OPNET Simulation Tool provides a convenient way to specify simulation parameters and execute simulations from within the OPNET environment.

1. Open the Simulation Tool by clicking the **Simulation Tool** tool button.

2. Specify the simulator parameters. To specify simulation parameters in the Simulation Tool, you first create a simulation object and then modify the objects attributes. Most of the parameters are model-independent, such as the simulation duration or the random number seed; but specific models may have attributes that were left undefined when the model was created. In our example, the undefined attributes are the promoted **interarrival args**, **pksize args**, and **queue service rate**.

3. Activate the **Create Simulation Set Object** action button and place an object anywhere in the tool window.

4. Open the attribute dialog box of the simulation set object by right-clicking the icon.

5. Change the attributes on the left of the dialog box as follows:

   - Name: **mm1_net**, Network: **mm1_net**, Probe file: **mm1_probe**, Vector file: **mm1_out**, Seed: **431**, Duration: **4000**, Update intvl: **250**.

mm1_out is a new file, used to store the statistics generated during the simulation. The seed can be any positive integer. Duration is the number of simulated seconds the simulation will run. **Update intvl** is the number of simulated seconds between progress updates in the message display.

6. Change the attributes in the table on the right of the dialog box as follows:

   - Click the **Add** button to build the list of available attributes. The **add attributes box** displays.
   - Click in the **Add?** column to select each attribute. You will need to click three times, once in each row.

     The displayed attributes were left undefined when the model was created. Leaving them undefined in the model allows you to specify the values at simulation time so that values can be changed without changing the model.
   - Close the Add Attributes dialog box by clicking the **OK** button.
   - Set **interarrival args** to 1.0, **queue service rate** to 9600, **pk size args** to 9000.

7. Close the simulation attributes dialog box by clicking the **OK** button.

8. Activate the **Write Simulation Sequence** action button. Name the file **mm1_sim**.

9. Activate the **Execute Simulation Sequence** action button.

An audible beep occurs when the simulation is complete.

2.2.5   Analyzing the Results

The Analysis Tool offers the capability of representing simulation statistics in a variety of two-dimensional graph formats. Statistics monitored during the course of a single simulation are written to an *output vector* file. An output vector file contains *time series* data for each of the statistics. The default name of an output file is based on the corresponding simulation.

1. Open the Analysis Tool by clicking the **Analysis Tool** tool button.

2. Activate the **Output Vector File** action button.

3. Select **mm1_out** from the menu of output vector files that pops up.

   The simplest possible graph is that of a single vector.

4. Activate the create **Single Vector Panel** action button.

5. Select **mean_delay** from the menu of available vectors that pops up.

6. Specify where you want to place the panel by dragging a box in the tool window. The graph appears in the panel as in Figure 2.3.

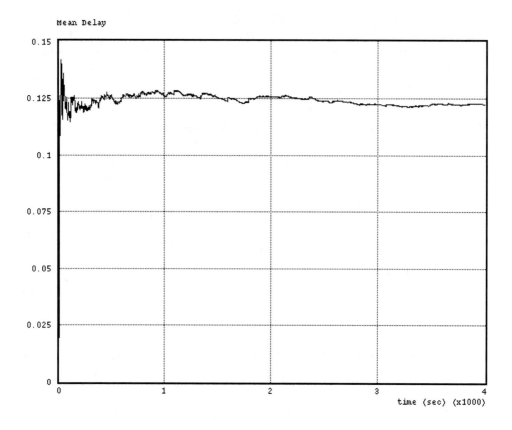

Figure 2.3. Mean Delay versus Time: M/M/1 Queue.

Answer the following questions:

1. Why do you observe a big change in the mean delay in the time interval 0–1000 sec?

2. Recall the attributes set for the simulator. Packets averaging 9000 bits in length arrive on average once every second. What is the value of mean arrival rate in packets/sec?

3. What is the value of the mean service requirement?

4. Find the theoretical mean delay from the formula $\overline{W} = 1/(\mu C - \lambda)$.

5. From the graph, read the ending mean delay. Compare the value with the one given by the previous formula. Why do the two values differ?

Another statistic of interest is the **time-averaged queue size**. The menu of available output vectors used earlier included a statistic called **mean_pksize**. This statistic computes a simple running average queue size with any previously accumulated sum whether a queue insertion or a removal event occurs, and then dividing by the number of events. This statistic does not represent the **time-averaged queue size**. To properly obtain the statistic, we should get the integral of the **mean_pksize** vector and divide it by the elapsed time. The desired time-averaged queue size may be obtained by applying the Analysis Tool *filter* to the existing **pksize** vector.

1. Activate the **Execute Filter Model** action button.

2. Select **time_average** from the menu of available filters that pops up

3. In the **Enter Value** box, type **time averaged pksize** and press <Return>.

4. Select **pksize** from the menu of available vectors that pops up.

5. Specify where you want the panel by dragging a box in the tool window. The filtered graph appears in the panel.

Compare the **time averaged pksize final value** with the expected value obtained by the traditional formula: $\rho/(1 - \rho)$, where $\rho = \lambda/\mu C$. What do you observe?

It is often desirable to have multiple vectors plotted in the same graph. Let us try an example.

1. Activate the **Create Multi-Vector Panel** button.

2. Select panel contents from the menu of available traces that pops up.

3. Click the **time-averaged pksize** panel to select the first vector.

4. Select **pksize** from the menu of available vectors to select the second vector in the graph.

5. Close the dialog box by clicking the **Close** button.

6. Place the graph on the panel. The multiple vector graph appears in the panel. The new panel displays two traces. The **pksize** trace shows the instantaneous number of packets in the queue during the course of the simulation. The **time-averaged pksize** trace depicts the average number of packets in the queue over time.

2.3 Extensions

If desired, return to the Simulation Tool and change the **interarrival args** or the **service rate** or the **average pksize** values and re-execute the simulation. Then compare the results with the values observed. But remember to change the name of the output vector file if you want to retain the results from previous simulations.

Chapter 3

Automatic Request Repeat (ARQ) Protocols

In this set of experiments we will study the design of the data link layer. The study deals with the performance of algorithms for achieving reliable, efficient communication between two adjacent machines at the data link layer. The term *adjacent* refers to the fact that the machines are physically connected by a communication channel that acts conceptually as a wire (for example, telephone line, coaxial cable, etc.) [1]. The essential property of a channel that makes it "wire-like" is that the bits are delivered in exactly the same order as they are sent.

The function of the data link layer is to provide services to the network layer. The data link layer has a number of specific functions to carry out. These functions include providing a well-defined interface to the network layer, determining how the bits of the physical layer are grouped into frames, dealing with transmission errors, and regulating the flow of frames so that slow receivers are not swamped by fast senders.

Communication channels are prone to errors and loss of data. Data loss occurs for a number of reasons: buffer overflow, noise in the system, faulty equipment. Data errors can be detected in the data link layer with the use of error detection codes. Error detection is combined with retransmission of information to ensure high reliability over channels that are prone to errors.

Automatic Request protocols (ARQ) detect frames with errors, and request the transmitting node to repeat the information of those frames. There are two main aspects of any retransmission protocol: correctness and efficiency. Correctness examines two questions: Does the protocol succeed in delivering each frame exactly once, without errors? and Does the protocol ensure that frames are received in the right order? The second aspect of any retransmission protocol is efficiency, i.e., how much of the link transmitting capacity is wasted by unnecessary waiting and retransmission of frames.

The best-known ARQ protocols are *Stop-and-Wait*, *Go-Back-N*, and *Selective-Repeat*, which are used in a variety of standardized data link protocols. For example, HDLC, developed by the International Organization for Standardization (ISO), is essentially a *Go-Back-N* ARQ protocol.

3.1   Objectives

In this set of simulation experiments, we will study the behavior of the *Stop-and-Wait*, *Go-Back-N*, and *Selective-Repeat* protocols. The objectives of the lab are:

1. To look at various parameters that characterize the performance of ARQ protocols.

2. To access via simulation the performance of *Stop-and-Wait*, *Go-Back-N*, and *Selective-Repeat* protocols. The throughput and link utilization characteristics of each protocol depend on several parameters, such as packet lengths; packet timeout, i.e., the amount of time the process will wait for an acknowledgment before retransmission; link propagation delay; etc. The task is to observe the performance of each of the protocols with varying input parameters.

3. To compare the performance of the schemes under various conditions.

3.2   Preparation

Answer the following questions:

1. Using a time diagram, describe how *Stop-and-Wait* operates using positive acknowledgments and timeouts.

2. Using a time diagram, describe how *Go-Back-N* operates using negative acknowledgments, positive acknowledgments, and timeouts.

3. Using a time diagram, describe how *Selective-Repeat* operates using negative acknowledgments, positive acknowledgments, and timeouts.

4. Explain how we can set the window parameters of the *Selective-Repeat* ARQ protocol so that it behaves like the *Stop-and-Wait* protocol and the *Go-Back-N* protocol.

3.3   Stop-and-Wait

A network has already been created for you. This network implements the *Stop-and-Wait* protocol with positive acknowledgments and timeouts. It consists of two nodes—Transmitter (**stop_wait** node model) and Receiver (**stop_wait** node model)—and a duplex link (**sw_link** link model) between them. The link is used to transport both the data frames and the acknowledgments. We assume that the transmitter always has frames to transmit. This allows the maximum throughput to be generated. To find out more about this network, use the following steps:

1. Open the Network Editor by clicking the **Network Editor** tool button.

2. Activate the **Read Network Model** action button.

3. Read the model named **stop_wait** from the list of available models that pops up.

4. Right-click the transmitter, receiver, and link object icons to view their attributes.

5. For each of the transmitter, receiver, and link objects, list the attributes that are promoted to the simulation level. Define each of the attributes.

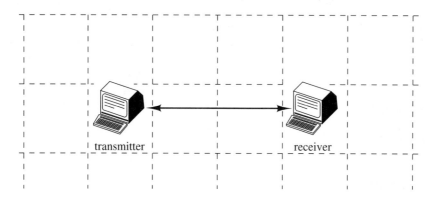

Figure 3.1. Stop-and-Wait Protocol.

3.3.1   Specify Probes

A number of statistics will be monitored during simulation. These have been selected using the Probe Editor. A probe file has already been created for you. To find out more about the collected statistics, use the following steps:

1. Open the Probe Editor by clicking the **Probe Editor** button.

2. Activate the **Read Probe Model** action button.

3. Read the probe file **stop_wait_probes** from the menu that pops up.

4. View the statistics that will be collected during the simulation by clicking each of the seven available probes. List the statistics that will be monitored during simulation as in Table 3.1.

Statistic Name	Units	Description
Offered Load	bits/sec	Average rate of traffic transmitted to the data link layer by the network layer
⋮	⋮	⋮

Table 3.1. Monitored Statistics for the Stop-and-Wait Experiments.

Note the two attribute probes that record the propagation delay and packet timeout. Attribute statistics are used to record the values of attributes during multiple passes of the simulation. They are used for plotting the value of a statistic versus the attribute.

3.3.2   Prepare the Simulation Set Object

To specify simulation parameters in the Simulation Tool, you must first create a simulation object and then modify the object's attributes. Such an object has been created for you and is stored in the file **stop_wait_sim**. Several parameters must be entered before the simulation can begin. To set the parameters, use the following steps:

1. Open the Simulation Editor by left-clicking the **Simulation** button.

2. Activate the **Read Simulation Model** action button.

3. Read the file **stop_wait_sim** from the menu that pops up.

4. Open the attribute dialog box of the simulation object by right-clicking the icon.

5. Change the attributes on the left of the dialog box as follows:

   - **Network:** stop_wait, **Probe file:** stop_wait_probes, **Vector file:** stop_wait, **Scalar file:** stop_wait.
   - Select as **Seed** any positive integer, for example 513.
   - Set the **Duration of the simulation** to 10000 (any duration above 2000 will achieve a steady state for the system's simulation).

   Remember to press <Return> after typing data into a text entry box.

6. Change the attributes on the right of the dialog box as follows:

   - Click the **Add Attributes** button to build the list of available attributes.
   - Click in the **Add?** column to select each attribute. Add the attributes *Interarrival Time, Packet Timeout, Delay, BER* (Bit Error Rate), *Packet Size.* You must click five times, once in each row.
   - Close the **Add Attributes** box by clicking the **OK** button.

7. Save the simulation sequence by activating the **Write Simulation Sequence** action button and overwrite the existing **stop_wait_sim** file.

3.3.3   Simulation Execution and Results Analysis

We will study the effect of packet size, link propagation delay, and packet timeout to the throughput, link utilization, and number of packet retransmissions. We start by studying the effect of packet size on the protocol performance.

Packet Size

Several parameters must be entered before the simulation can begin.

1. Open the attribute dialog box of the simulation object by right-clicking the icon.

2. Change the attributes on the right of the dialog box as follows:

- **Interarrival Time:** 1.0. The interarrival time allows the interarrival between generated packets in the transmitter to be varied. A smaller value of interarrival time corresponds to increasing offered traffic.

- **Packet Timeout:** 1.0. The packet timeout defines the amount of time the process will wait for an acknowledgment before retransmission.

- **Delay:** 0.0.

- **BER (Bit Error Rate):** 0.00002.

- Select 8 values for the **Packet Size** in the range 50 to 10000 bits. For example: 50, 100, 1000, 3500, 4000, 5000, 8192, 10000. To select multiple values for a simulation attribute, follow these steps:

  - The **Values** action button is highlighted in the bottom of the panel. Left-click the **Values** action button.
  - Enter the selected values for the packet size, one in each row (first column). Do not forget to press <Return> every time you write a value.
  - Click **OK** to close the Values Panel.

3. Activate the **save vector file for each run in the set** radio button. This allows you to store the simulation traces in different vector files for different packet sizes. In this lab, the results of the simulator traces will be stored in the vector files **stop_wait_1** to **stop_wait_8**.

4. Click **OK** to close the simulation object.

5. Activate the **Execute Simulation Sequence** action button. A simulation sequence composed of many runs may be time-consuming to execute; this dialog box gives you the option of deferring the process.

6. OPNET displays messages to show when the simulation is complete.

Analysis

We will use the Analysis Tool to evaluate the results of the simulation. First open the Analysis Tool by left-clicking the **Analysis Tool** tool button.

Throughput versus Packet Size

1. Left-click the **Open Output Vector File** action button and select **stop_wait_7**. Although the display is not changed, the vector file is read.

2. Left-click the **Create Single Vector Panel** action button and select **Throughput**(bits/sec) from the pop-up list.

3. Draw the panel by drawing a box in the tool window. First click the location for the upper left corner, then drag to the lower right corner.

4. The displayed graph corresponds to the throughput of the protocol, over time, for the first selected (in the simulator) packet size value as it is shown in Figure 3.2.

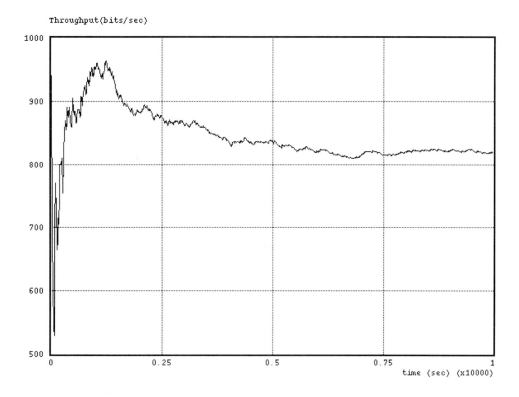

Figure 3.2. Throughput versus Time: Stop and Wait Protocol.

5. Right-click the panel to display the Edit Panel dialog box.

6. Click the **Trace Info** button at the bottom of the dialog box. A text pad appears, showing information about the vector.

7. Collect the values of packet size and throughput final value and record it in a table.

8. Repeat the previous 7 steps for the rest of the vector files **stop_wait_2** to **stop_wait_8** and collect the data of interest (packet size and throughput final values), and record them in a table, as in Table 3.2.

9. When you finish collecting the data, press the **Global Action** button and clear the Analysis Tool of all the graphs.

From the collected data, plot the Throughput versus Packet Size. What do you observe? What happens to throughput when the packet size increases? Can you give an intuitive explanation?

Vector File	Packet Size	Final Throughput Value
$\vdots$	$\vdots$	$\vdots$
stop_wait_7	8192 bits	826 bits/sec

Table 3.2. Throughput versus Packet Size: Stop and Wait Protocol.

Link Utilization versus Packet Size
Repeat the same procedure as above to collect the required data to plot link utilization versus packet size. The steps are exactly the same as for the throughput case. Just select, in step 2, the **Link Utilization** trace instead of the **Throughput**.

From the collected data, plot the Link Utilization versus Packet Size. What do you observe? Can you give an explanation?

Number of Retransmissions versus Packet Size
Repeat the same procedure as above to collect the required data to plot the number of retransmissions versus packet size. The steps are exactly the same as for the throughput case. Just select, in step 2, the **Number of Retransmissions** trace instead of the **Throughput**.

From the collected data, plot the **Number of Retransmissions** versus **Packet Size**. What do you observe? Can you give an explanation? Why does the Number of Retransmissions increase as the packet size increases?

Propagation Delay

1. Return to the Simulation Tool.

2. Open the attribute dialog box of the simulation set object by right-clicking the icon.

3. Change the attributes on the right of the dialog box as follows:

   - **Interarrival Time:** 1.0, **Packet Timeout:** 1.0, **Packet Size:** 4000, **BER:** 0.0002.
   - Select 8 values for the **Delay** in the range 0.01 to 1.0 sec. For example: 0.01, 0.1, 0.2, 0.35, 0.5, 0.7, 0.9, 1.0.

4. Change the attribute **Scalar file** on the left of the dialog box to **stop_wait**.

5. When you are finished with the definition, close the dialog box.

6. Activate the **Delete Models** action button. A list of deletable file types appears.

7. Select the **Output Scalar** item. A list of available **output scalar files** appears.

8. If the list contains the **output scalar file** stop_wait, select the entry to delete the file.

This simulation produces scalar results. Thus, an **output scalar file** must be specified where these results accumulate from successive simulations. If the **output scalar file** stop_wait does not exist when the simulation sequence begins, one will be created so that scalar results may be recorded. If the file already exists, the simulation executables will append their scalar results to this file. To avoid viewing obsolete results that already exist in a similarly named file, the **output scalar file** stop_wait must be deleted if it exists.

9. Close the open dialog boxes.

10. Activate the **Execute Simulation Sequence** action button.

11. OPNET displays messages to show when the simulation is complete.

Analysis

1. Open the Analysis Tool.

2. Activate the **Output Scalar File** action button.

3. Select **stop_wait** from the menu of statistics vectors that pops up.

4. Activate the **Create Scalar Panel** action button.

5. Select the Abscissa **Propagation Delay** first, then select the ordinate variable **Throughput (bits/sec)** from the menu of available scalars that pops up.

6. Click **OK** and place the panel anywhere within the workspace by drawing a box where you want the panel to be.

7. Repeat the above procedure to also plot **Link Utilization** versus **Propagation Delay**, and **Number of Retransmissions** versus **Propagation Delay**.

What happens to the throughput, link utilization, and number of retransmissions as the propagation delay increases? Can you explain the observed results?

Packet Timeout

1. Return to the Simulation Tool.

2. Change the simulation attributes as follows:

   - **Interarrival Time:** 1.0, **Propagation Delay:** 0.0, **Packet Size:** 4000.
   - Select 8 values for the **Packet Timeout:** in the range 0.1 to 10 sec. For example: 0.1, 0.5, 0.8, 1.0, 3.0, 5.0, 8.0, 10.0.

3. Change the attribute **Scalar File** on the left of the dialog box to **stop_wait_t**.

4. If the output scalar file **stop_wait_t** exists, remove it with the Delete Models operation.

5. Execute the simulation.

Analysis

1. Open the Analysis Tool.

2. Plot **Throughput (bits/sec)** versus **Packet Timeout**.

3. Plot **Link Utilization** versus **Packet Timeout**, and **Number of Retransmissions** versus **Packet Timeout**.

What happens to throughput, link utilization, and number of retransmissions as the packet timeout duration increases? Can you explain the observed results?

A summary of the Stop-and-Wait protocol simulation experiment parameters and results is given in Tables 3.3 and 3.4.

Experiment	Simulation Parameters
Effect of Packet Size *simulation file:* stop_wait_sim	Interarrival Time: 1.0 sec Packet Timeout: 1.0 sec Delay: 0.0 sec BER: 0.0002 Packet Size: 50–10000 bits *select 8 values in the range*
Effect of Propagation Delay *simulation file:* stop_wait_sim	Interarrival Time: 1.0 sec Packet Timeout: 1.0 sec Delay: 0.01 - 1.0 sec BER: 0.0002 Packet Size: 4000 bits *select 8 values in the range*
Effect of Propagation Delay *simulation file:* stop_wait_sim	Interarrival Time: 1.0 sec Packet Timeout: 0.1–10 sec Delay: 0.0 sec BER: 0.0002 Packet Size: 4000 bits *select 8 values in the range*

Table 3.3. Simulation Parameters for the Stop-and-Wait Experiments.

Experiment	Simulation Results
Effect of Packet Size *output vector files:* stop_wait_1 - stop_wait_8	Throughput (b/s) vs. Packet Size Link Utilization vs. Packet Size Number of Retransmissions vs. Packet Size
Effect of Propagation Delay *output scalar file:* stop_wait	Throughput (b/s) vs. Propagation Delay Link Utilization vs. Propagation Delay Number of Retransmissions vs. Propagation Delay
Effect of Packet Timeout *output scalar file:* stop_wait_t	Throughput (b/s) vs. Packet Timeout Link Utilization vs. Packet Timeout Number of Retransmissions vs. Packet Timeout

Table 3.4. Simulation Results for the Stop-and-Wait Experiments.

3.4 Go-Back-N

A network has already been created for you. This network implements the *Go-Back-N* protocol with negative and positive acknowledgments, as well as timeouts. It consists of two nodes— *node_0* (**swp_node_base** node model) and *node_1* (**swp_node_base** node model), and a duplex link (**sw_link** link model) between them. To find out more about this network, use the same steps as in the *Stop-Wait* case, but this time open the file **go_back_n** to read the network model.

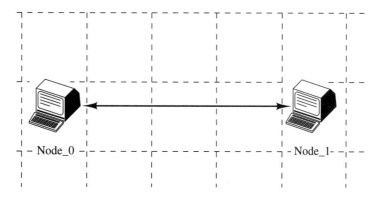

Figure 3.3. Go-Back-N Protocol.

3.4.1   Specify Probes

A number of statistics will be monitored during simulation. These were selected using the Probe Editor. A probe file has already been created for you. To find out more about the collected statistics, follow the same steps as in the *Stop-Wait* experiments (Section 3.3.1), but this time open the **go_back_n_probes** file to view the probes and monitored statistics.

3.4.2   Prepare the Simulation Set Object

To specify simulation parameters in the Simulation Tool, you must first create a simulation set object and then modify the object's attributes. Such an object has been created for you and stored in the file **go_back_n_sim**. Use similar steps as in the **stop-and-wait** case (Section 3.3.2) to modify the simulation object for the **go-back-n** case.

1. Change the attributes of the simulation object as follows:

   - Network: **go_back_n**, Probe file: *go_back_n probes*, Vector file: **go_back_n**.

Experiment	Simulation Parameters
Effect of Packet Size *simulation file:* go_back_n_sim	Interarrival Time: 1.0 sec Packet Timeout: 1.0 sec Delay: 0.0 sec BER: 0.0002 Packet Size: 50–10000 bits *select 8 values in the range*
Effect of Propagation Delay *simulation file:* go_back_n_sim	Interarrival Time: 1.0 sec Packet Timeout: 1.0 sec Delay: 0.01–1.0 sec BER: 0.0002 Packet Size: 4000 bits *select 8 values in the range*
Effect of Packet Timeout *simulation file:* go_back_n_sim	Interarrival Time: 1.0 sec Packet Timeout: 0.1–10 sec Delay: 0.0 sec BER: 0.0002 Packet Size: 4000 bits *select 8 values in the range*

Table 3.5. Simulation Parameters for the Go-Back-N Experiments.

- Select as **Seed** any positive integer; for example, 513.

- Set the **Duration** of the simulation to 10000.

Remember to press <Return> after typing data into a text entry box.

2. Add the Packet Size, Delay, Packet Timeout, and BER attributes to the simulation set object as in the **stop-and-wait** protocol experiments.

3. Save the modified simulation sequence into the **go_back_n_sim** file.

3.4.3   Simulation Execution and Results Analysis

As in the **stop-and-wait** protocol, we will study the effect of packet size, link propagation delay, and packet timeout on the throughput, link utilization, and number of packet retransmissions. We will perform three sets of simulation experiments, one for each of the parameters that affects the performance of the protocol. The simulation experiments are similar to the ones performed for the **stop-and-wait** protocol. In Table 3.5 we summarize the simulation parameters and the collected statistics for each of the experiments. The simulation steps are similar to the ones described in Section 3.3.3.

Analysis

We will use the Analysis Tool to evaluate the results of the simulation. Using similar steps as in the performance analysis of the *Stop-and-Wait* protocol (Section 3.3.3), plot the simulation results that are listed in Table 3.6.

Experiment	Simulation Results
Effect of Packet Size *output vector files:* go_back_n1 - go_back_n8	Throughput (b/s) vs. Packet Size Link Utilization vs. Packet Size Number of Retransmissions vs. Packet Size
Effect of Propagation Delay *output scalar file:* go_back_n	Throughput (b/s) vs. Propagation Delay Link Utilization vs. Propagation Delay Number of Retransmissions vs. Propagation Delay
Effect of Packet Timeout *output scalar file:* go_back_n_t	Throughput (b/s) vs. Packet Timeout Link Utilization vs. Packet Timeout Number of Retransmissions vs. Packet Timeout

Table 3.6. Simulation Results for the Go-Back-N Experiments.

Packet Size

1. *Throughput versus Packet Size:* From the collected data, plot the **Throughput** versus **Packet Size**. What do you observe? What happens to throughput when the packet size increases? Can you give an explanation?

2. *Link Utilization versus Packet Size:* Use the collected data to plot the **Link Utilization** versus **Packet Size**. What do you observe? Can you give an explanation?

3. *Number of Retransmissions versus Packet Size:* Plot the **Number of Retransmissions** versus **Packet Size**. What do you observe? Can you give an explanation? Why does the number of retransmissions increase as the packet size increases?

Propagation Delay

What happens to the throughput, link utilization, and number of retransmissions as the propagation delay increases? Can you explain the observed results?

Packet Timeout

What happens to the throughput, link utilization, and number of retransmissions as the packet timeout duration increases? Can you explain the observed results?

3.5   Selective Repeat

A network has already been created for you. This network implements the Selective-Repeat protocol with positive and negative acknowledgments as well as timeouts. It consists of two nodes—*node_0* (**swp_node_base** node model) and *node_1* (**swp_node_base** node model)—and a duplex link (**sw_link** link model) between them. To find out more about this network use the same steps as in the *Stop-Wait* case, but this time open the file **sel_rep** to read the network model. Note the promoted attribute **Window Size**.

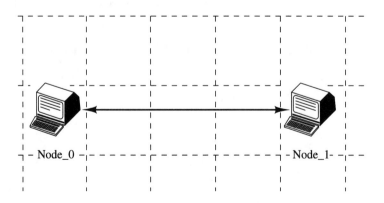

Figure 3.4. Selective Repeat Protocol.

3.5.1 Specify Probes

A number of statistics will be monitored during simulation. These had been selected using the Probe Editor. A probe file has already been created for you. To find out more about the collected statistics follow the same steps as in the *Stop-Wait* experiments, but this time open the **sel_rep_probes** file to view the probes and monitored statistics.

3.5.2 Prepare the Simulation Set Object

The simulation set object for the Selective Repeat protocol experiments is stored in the file **sel_rep_sim.** Several parameters must be modified before the simulation can begin.

1. Change the attributes of the simulation object as follows:

   - **Network:** sel_rep, **Probe File:** sel_rep_probes, **Vector File:** sel_rep.
   - Select as **Seed** any positive integer, for example 513.
   - Set the **Duration** of the simulation to 2000 (any duration above 1000 will achieve a steady state of the simulation).

   Remember to press < Return > after typing data into a text entry box.

2. Add the attributes Interarrival Time, Packet Size, Delay, and Packet Timeout, as well as the attribute Window Size. The resulting simulation set object is given in Figure 3.5.

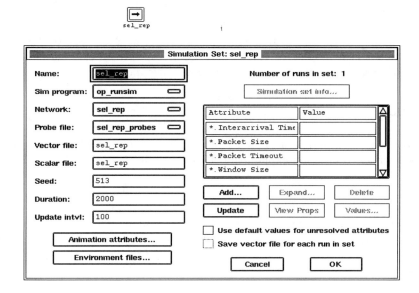

Figure 3.5. Simulation Set Object: Selective Repeat Protocol.

3. Save the simulation sequence in the existing **sel_rep_sim** file.

3.5.3   Simulation Execution and Results Analysis

As in the previous experiments, for the *Stop-and-Wait* and *Go-Back-N* protocols, we will study the effect of packet size, link propagation delay, packet timeout to the throughput, link utilization, and number of packet retransmissions. In Table 3.7 we summarize the simulation parameters and the collected statistics for each of the experiments. The simulation steps are similar to the ones described in Section 3.3.3.

Analysis

We will use the Analysis Tool to evaluate the results of the simulation. Using similar steps as in the performance analysis of the *Stop-and-Wait* protocol (Section 3.3.3), plot the simulation results that are listed in Table 3.8.

Packet Size

1. *Throughput versus Packet Size:* From the collected data, plot the **Throughput** versus **Packet Size**. What do you observe? What happens to throughput when the packet size increases? Can you give an explanation?

2. *Link Utilization versus Packet Size:* Use the collected data to plot the **Link Utilization** versus **Packet Size**. What do you observe? Can you give an explanation?

3. *Number of Retransmissions versus Packet Size:* Plot the **Number of Retransmissions** versus **Packet Size**. What do you observe? Can you give an explanation? Why does the number of retransmissions increase as the packet size increases?

Propagation Delay

What happens to the throughput, link utilization, and number of retransmissions as the propagation delay increases? Can you explain the observed results?

Packet Timeout

What happens to the throughput, link utilization, and number of retransmissions as the packet timeout duration increases? Can you explain the observed results?

Window Size

What happens to the throughput, link utilization, and number of retransmissions as the window size increases? Can you explain the observed results?

Experiment	Simulation Parameters
Effect of Packet Size *simulation file:* sel_rep_sim	Interarrival Time: 1.0 sec Packet Timeout: 1.0 sec Delay: 0.0 sec BER: 0.0002 Packet Size: 50–10000 bits Window Size: 8 *select 8 values in the range*
Effect of Propagation Delay *simulation file:* sel_rep_sim	Interarrival Time: 1.0 sec Packet Timeout: 1.0 sec Delay: 0.01–1.0 sec *select 8 values in the range* BER: 0.0002 Packet Size: 8192 bits Window Size: 8
Effect of Packet Timeout *simulation file:* sel_rep_sim	Interarrival Time: 1.0 Packet Timeout: 0.1–10 sec *select 8 values in the range* Delay: 0.0 sec BER: 0.0002 Packet Size: 8192 bits Window Size: 8
Effect of Window Size *simulation file:* sel_rep_sim	Interarrival Time: 1.0 sec Packet Timeout: 0.1–10 sec Delay: 0.0 sec BER: 0.0002 Packet Size: 8192 bits Window Size: 1, 8, 16, 32, 64, 128

Table 3.7. Simulation Parameters for the Selective Repeat Experiments.

Experiment	Simulation Results
Effect of Packet Size *output vector files:* sel_rep_1 - sel_rep_8	Throughput (b/s) vs. Packet Size Link Utilization vs. Packet Size Number of Retransmissions vs. Packet Size
Effect of Propagation Delay *output scalar file:* sel_rep	Throughput (b/s) vs. Propagation Delay Link Utilization vs. Propagation Delay Number of Retransmissions vs. Propagation Delay
Effect of Packet Timeout *output scalar file:* sel_rep_t	Throughput (b/s) vs. Packet Timeout Link Utilization vs. Packet Timeout Number of Retransmissions vs. Packet Timeout

Table 3.8. Simulation Results for the Selective Repeat Experiments.

3.6   Conclusions

Use the data gathered from your simulations to answer the following:

1. Plot throughput versus packet size for each ARQ scheme. What happens to throughput when the packet size increases?

2. What is the maximum throughput of each ARQ protocol? For which packet size is it achieved?

3. How does the propagation delay affect throughput?

4. How does packet timeout affect throughput?

5. Plot throughput(bits/sec) versus link utilization for each ARQ scheme. Which scheme gives the lowest link utilization for a given throughput? Which scheme gives the maximum? Can you give an explanation for the observed results?

6. What happens to throughput when utilization approaches 100%?

References

[1] Andrew S. Tanenbaum, *Computer Networks*, 3rd Ed., Englewood Cliffs, NJ: Prentice Hall, 1996.

Chapter 4

Multiple Access Protocols

Networks, in general, can be divided into two broad categories: those using point-to-point connections and those using broadcast channels [1]. In the broadcast channel case, there is competition for the use of the channel between two or more stations. In the literature, broadcast channels are referred to as multiaccess channels, or random-access channels [1], [2], [3].

Multiple access protocols are implemented primarily in Local Area Networks (LANs). Today's personal computers and workstations are connected by Local Area Networks (LANs), which use a multiaccess channel as the basis of their communication. Examples of popular LANs are Ethernet and Token Passing Ring. Ethernet is an example of a random-access scheme, while Token Passing Ring is an example of a scheduled scheme.

The genesis of the random-access technique is the ALOHA protocol developed at the University of Hawaii in the 1970s. The initial ALOHA protocol (Pure ALOHA) was later extended to the slotted ALOHA scheme. Another popular random-access protocol is the Carrier Sensing Multiple Access (CSMA) scheme, which was developed by XEROX Parc. Ethernet uses an extension of CSMA, called CSMA-CD, that is a CSMA with collision detection.

On the other hand, ring networks have existed for many years and have been used for both Local Area and Wide Area networks. Token Ring became popular when IBM used it as its LAN. Token Ring uses a form of scheduled transmissions relying on a technique called *token passing*.

One of the major problems in multiaccess protocols is to determine who goes next on a multiaccess layer for transmission. The transmission medium is shared by a community of users, in a distributed way, with all stations sharing responsibility to arbitrate or to coordinate the access to the medium. Typically, the information from a user is broadcast into the medium and all the stations attached to the medium can listen to all of the transmissions. There is a potential for user transmissions interfering with other users, and so a method must be employed to prevent or minimize such interference. In this lab we will discuss different approaches to medium access control.

4.1 Objectives

In this lab we will study several multiaccess protocols. We will look at the Pure ALOHA, CSMA 1-persistent, CSMA-CD, and Token Passing Ring protocols. The objectives are:

- To study the various parameters that characterize each of the multiaccess protocols.

- To assess via simulation the performance of ALOHA, CSMA, CSMA-CD, and Token Ring multiaccess protocols and to study the throughput and delay characteristics of each of them.

- To compare the performance of the schemes under various conditions.

4.2   Preparation

From your textbook, answer the following questions:

1. What is the maximum throughput of the pure ALOHA scheme? State clearly all the assumptions needed.

2. Rank the protocols in terms of end-to-end delay under light and heavy load conditions. Justify your answer.

3. Rank the protocols in terms of throughput under light and heavy load conditions. Justify your answer.

4.3   Aloha

A network has already been created for you that models an **aloha** System. The network consists of a multitap bus, 20 transmitting nodes **node_1–node_20** (**cct_tx** node model) that generate and send packets, and one receiver node, **node_0** (**ccc_rx** node model), that will perform network monitoring. The system provides no coordination among the users or any ability for stations to know what is happening on the bus while transmission is taking place, i.e., no **carrier sense** capability. Simultaneous transmissions by two or more transmitting nodes (sources) result in a collision and garbling of all overlapping transmissions. The **Aloha** network model is stored in the file **aloha**. To learn more about the model, use the Network Editor to open the network model file **aloha**.

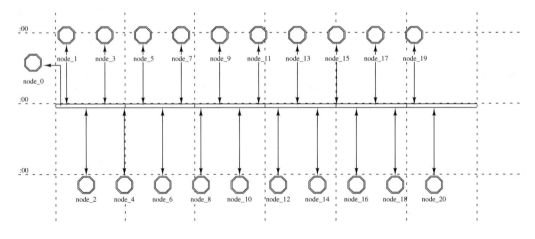

Figure 4.1. Aloha Network.

4.3.1   Prepare the Simulation Set Object

A generic simulation set object has been created for you, and is stored in the file **aloha_sim**.

1. Set the parameters of the simulation set object as follows:

   - **Network:** aloha_net, **Probe file:** NONE, **Scalar file:** aloha.

     The **Aloha** simulation set object does not require a probe file. However, because the simulation produces scalar results, an *output scalar file* must be specified where these results accumulate from successive simulations. If the **output scalar file aloha** exists, remove it with the Delete Models operation.

   - Select as **Seed** any positive number, for example 11.

   - Set the **Duration** of the simulator to 20000 and **Update intvl** to 100.

2. Add the attributes gen interarrival args, max packet count, and gen pksize to the simulation set object.

3. Save the simulation set object in the **aloha_sim** file.

4.3.2   Simulation Execution and Results Analysis

The goal of the simulation is to observe how the performance of the **Aloha** protocol varies as a function of the channel traffic. We will study the effect of channel traffic to **throughput** and **end-to-end delay**. The simulation **interarrival time** input parameter will be varied in this simulation sequence to produce different levels of traffic and, hence, different levels of throughput and end-to-end packet delay. A reasonable level of resolution will be achieved by executing twelve simulations, each with a different **interarrival time**. Several parameters must be entered before the simulations can begin.

1. Open the attribute dialog box of the simulation set object and define the simulation sequence as follows:

   - Set **pk size** to 1024.

   - Set the values of the *interarrival args* attribute as 1000, 200, 150, 100, 80, 50, 35, 30, 25, 20, 18, 15.

     The generator's promoted mean value for interarrival time allows the simulation to be parameterized at run time. The simulation sequence attributes for the **aloha** model introduce packets into the network at successively faster rates. The generated packet length of **1024 bits** and the default **channel** 0 data rate of **1024 bits/sec** on the bus transmitter provide a convenient packet transmission time of $\tau = 1.0$ sec.

   - Set **max packet count** to 1000. Setting the **max packet count** to 1000 keeps the simulation duration relatively short by allowing each node to generate about 50 packets.

2. Execute the simulation sequence. OPNET runs the 12 simulations, displaying progress messages as they proceed.

Analysis

The channel throughput and the end-to-end delay as a function of traffic across the simulation sequence will be displayed in the **Analysis Tool**. Each simulation executed by the simulation sequence causes three scalar results to be recorded to the **output scalar file**.

1. Open the Analysis Tool.

2. Select **aloha** from the menu of available statistic vectors.

3. Plot the **Channel Throughput S** versus the **Channel Traffic G**. Verify that your plot is similar to the one in Figure 4.2.

4. Plot also the **End-to-End Delay** versus **Channel Traffic G**.

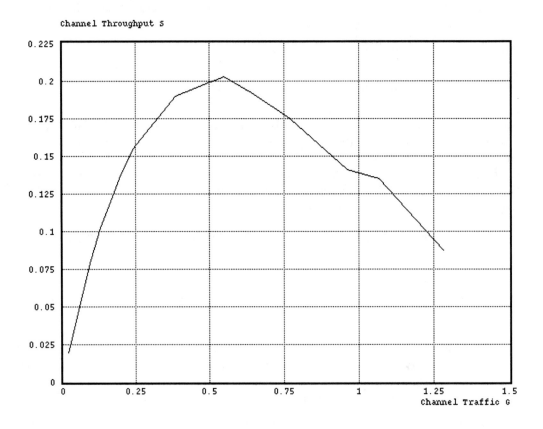

Figure 4.2. Channel Throughput versus Channel Traffic, Aloha Protocol.

Answer the following questions:

1. What is the theoretical maximum channel throughput of an **aloha** system?

2. What percentage of the submitted load does the channel carry at low traffic levels?

3. For which load is the maximum throughput achieved?

4. What happens to the throughput as the offered load increases? Can you give an intuitive explanation?

5. What happens to the end-to-end packet delay as the offered load increases? Can you give an explanation?

6. Do you observe any difference in the measured performance of this model and the analytical results? If yes, can you give an explanation? Which is more realistic, the simulation or the analytical results?

4.4   CSMA

A network has already been created for you that models a **CSMA** system. The network consists of a multitap bus (**cct_link** link model), 20 transmitting nodes (**node_1** to **node_20** (**csma_tx** node model) that generate and send packets, and one receiver node **node_0** (**cct_rx** node model) that will perform network monitoring. The system provides **carrier sense** capability, which requires a source node to sense the channel and determine that it is free before committing to a transmission. Because of finite signal propagation times, it is possible for a node to be transmitting before it detects an existing transmission signal. This results in some collisions. The CSMA network model is stored in the file **csma_a**. To learn more about the network, use the Network Editor to open the file **csma_a**.

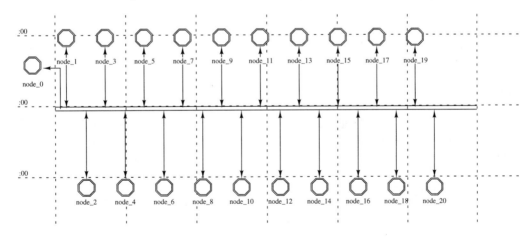

Figure 4.3. CSMA Protocol.

4.4.1   Prepare the Simulation Set Object

A generic simulator set object has been created for you, and is stored in the file **csma_sim**.

1. Set the parameters of the simulation set object as follows:

   - **Network:** csma_a, **Probe file:** NONE, **Scalar file:** csma.
   - Select as **Seed** any positive number; for example, 11.
   - Set the **Duration** of the simulation to 20000.

2. If the output scalar file **csma** exists, remove it with the Delete Models operation.

3. Save the simulation sequence in the **csma_sim** file.

4.4.2   Simulation Execution and Results Analysis

The goal of the simulation is to observe how the performance of the CSMA protocol varies as a function of the channel traffic. As in the **aloha** performance simulations, we will study here for **CSMA** the effect of channel traffic to the **throughput** and the **end-to-end delay**. The simulation **interarrival time** input parameter will be varied in this simulation sequence to produce different levels of traffic and, hence, different levels of throughput and end-to-end packet delay. A reasonable level of resolution will be achieved by executing 12 simulations, each with a different **interarrival time**.

1. Modify the simulation sequence as follows:

   - Set the values of the **interarrival args** attribute to 1000, 200, 150, 100, 80, 50, 35, 30, 25, 20, 18, 15.
   - Set **max packet count** to 1000.
   - Set **pk size** to 1024.

2. Execute the simulation sequence. OPNET runs the 12 simulations, displaying progress messages as they proceed.

Analysis

The channel throughput and the end-to-end delay as a function of traffic across the simulation sequence will be displayed in the **Analysis Tool**. Each simulation executed by the simulation sequence causes three scalar results to be recorded to the **output scalar file**. Open the Analysis Tool and plot:

1. The **Channel Throughput S** versus the **Channel Traffic G**. Verify that your plot looks like the one in Figure 4.4.

2. The **ETE Delay** versus **Channel Traffic G**.

Answer the following questions:

1. What is the theoretical maximum channel throughput of a CSMA system?

2. What percentage of the submitted load does the channel carry at low traffic levels (below 0.25)?

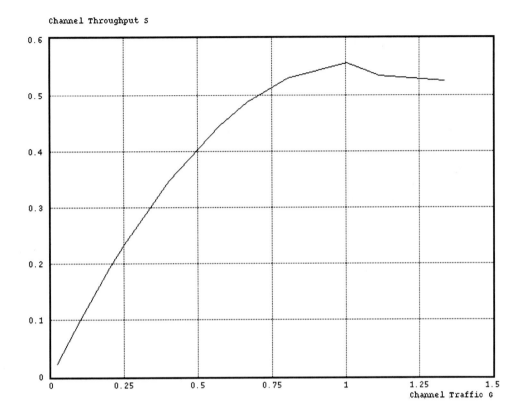

Figure 4.4. Channel Throughput versus Channel Traffic, CSMA Protocol.

3. For which load is the maximum throughput achieved?

4. For what value of the offered load does the throughput start to decrease? Why do you observe a decrease in the throughput above that offered load? Give an explanation.

5. What happens to end-to-end packet delay as the offered load increases? Do you observe anything "unusual" in the graph you plot? If yes, can you give an explanation? Can you provide a suggestion to improve the appearance of the graph?

6. Do you observe any difference in the measured performance of this model and the analytical results? If yes, can you give an explanation? Which is more realistic, the simulation results or the analytical results?

Comparison between ALOHA and CSMA

To compare the throughput performance of the ALOHA and CSMA protocols, it is easier to display both curves simultaneously on the same graph.

1. Plot the **Channel Throughput** versus **Channel Traffic** for the **aloha** system.

2. Plot also the **Channel Throughput** versus **Channel Traffic** for the **CSMA** system. Place the panels inside the workspace in such a way that both the **aloha** and **csma** graphs are at least partially visible.

3. To distinguish the graphs, label the **aloha** panel by following these steps:

   - Left-click Panel #0 if it is not the active panel.
   - Right-click the panel to open the **Edit Panel** dialog box.
   - Enter **Aloha** in the **Panel title** field and press <Return>. The panel formerly labeled panel #0 is now called Aloha.

4. Change the label of the **csma** panel (panel #1) to CSMA.

5. Activate the **Create Multiple-Vector Panel** action button.

6. Select **panel contents** from the menu of available traces that pops up, but do not close the menu.

7. Click the **CSMA** output scalar panel using the left mouse button to choose the first trace.

8. Select **panel contents** from the menu again, but do not close the menu.

9. Click the **aloha** output scalar panel using the left mouse button to choose the second trace.

10. Terminate the selection of multiple vectors by clicking the **Close** button.

11. Specify where you want the resulting analysis panel by drawing a box in the tool window. Both traces appear in the panel, with the two curves displayed in different colors.

Repeat similar steps to plot the vectors of the **ETE Delay** for the two protocols in a combined graph.

Answer the following questions:

1. What percent of throughput increase does the CSMA achieve over ALOHA in light and in heavy load conditions? Can you give an explanation?

2. What percent of delay decrease does the CSMA achieve over ALOHA in light and heavy load conditions? Can you give an explanation?

3. Plot the **Throughput** versus **ETE Delay** for the two protocols. What do you observe? Can you give an intuitive explanation?

4.5   Ethernet

A network model has already been created for you, and is stored in the **ethcoax_net** file. It consists of a multitap bus network populated by 8 nodes. The nodes employ the node model **ethcoax_station_base**. The network models a Carrier-Sense Multiple Access with Collision Detection (CSMA/CD) system. The CSMA/CD protocol is practiced by the commercial protocol *Ethernet*, and it is modeled by an OPNET supplied example model. To learn more about the system, open the **ethcoax_net** file.

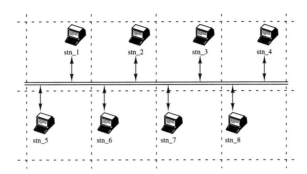

Figure 4.5. Ethernet Network.

4.5.1 Specify Probes

A number of statistics will be monitored during simulation. These must be selected using the Probe Editor. A probe file has already been created for you and stored in the **ethernet_probes** file. The following statistics will be monitored:

1. **S1 Specified Offered Load** (bits/sec). Represents the calculated load in bits/sec for the Ethernet generator in this node. **Calculation Method:** specified traffic generation rate multiplied by the mean data size.

2. **S1 Actual Load** (bits/sec): Represents the average rate of traffic submitted to the specified Ethernet layer (**S1 node**) by the next-higher layer in this node. *Calculation Method:* total bits submitted divided by the current simulation time.

3. **S1 Thoroughput**. Average bits per second forwarded to the next-higher layer by the specified Ethernet layer in this node (node S1). **Calculation Method**: number of bits forwarded divided by the current simulation time.

4. **S1 Utilization**. Represents a measure of consumption to date of an available channel bandwidth, where the value of **1.0** indicates full usage.

5. **S1 ETE Delay** (sec). Represents the end-to-end delay of frames accepted by the specified Ethernet layer in this node (**node S1**). Measured from the time a frame is submitted to the Ethernet layer of the remote node for transmission to the time the frame is received by this node.

6. **S1 Collision Count**. Represents the number of collisions encountered by the specified Ethernet layer in this node (node **S1**).

7. **Bus Utilization**. Represents a measure of the consumption to date of an available channel bandwidth, where a value of 1.0 indicates full usage.

8. **Bus Throughput**(bits/sec). Represents the average number of bits successfully received or transmitted by the receiver or transmitter channel per unit time, in bits/sec.

9. **Total Specified Offered Load**(bits/sec). Represents the calculated load in bits/sec for all Ethernet generators in the network. *Calculation Method:* sum of the specified loads for all Ethernet generators.

10. **Total Actual Load** (bits/sec). Represents the average rate of traffic submitted to all Ethernet layers in the network by the next-higher layers. *Calculation Method:* total bits submitted divided by the current simulation time.

11. **Ethernet Throughput** (bits/sec). Average bits/sec forward to the next-higher layers by all Ethernet layers in the network. *Calculation Method:* number of bits forwarded divided by the current simulation time.

12. **Ethernet ETE Delay** (sec). Represents the end-to-end delay of frames accepted by all Ethernet layers in the network. Measured from the time a frame is submitted to the Ethernet layer for transmission to the time the frame is received by the destination node.

4.5.2   Prepare the Simulation Set Object

A generic simulation set object has been created for you, and stored in the file **ethernet_sim**. Modify the parameters of the simulation set object as follows:

1. **Network:** ethcoax_net, **Probe file:** ethernet, **Vector file:** ethernet, **Scalar file:** ethernet.

2. Select as **Seed** any positive number; for example, 11.

3. Set the **Duration** of the simulation to 30 and the **Update intv** to 10.

4. Set the **Application Data Size** to 12,000, the **Application Start Time** to 5.0, and the **Application Traffic Generation Rate** to 30.

Save the simulation sequence in the **ethernet_sim** file, and with the simulation.

4.5.3   Simulation Execution and Result Analysis

The goal of the simulation is to observe how the performance of the **Ethernet** protocol varies as a function of the total offered traffic. The performance analysis of the **Ethernet** model will be approached in two different ways. First, we will analyze the performance of the protocol by observing traces of statistics as a function of time for a specific **Total Offered Load**; then we will study the effect of total offered traffic on the **throughput, end-to-end delay**, and **bus utilization** as the total offered load varies.

Trace Analysis at a Specific Total Offered Load

1. Open the Analysis Tool.

2. Plot the **S1 Utilization** versus time. Verify that the plot is similar to the one in Figure 4.6. Note that, because of their identical interarrival argument, the channel utilization of the 8 individual transmitters is fairly represented by one transmitter.

3. Plot also the statistics **S1 ETE Delay, S1 Collision Count, Bus Utilization, Bus Throughput, Ethernet Throughput**, and **Ethernet ETE Delay** versus time.

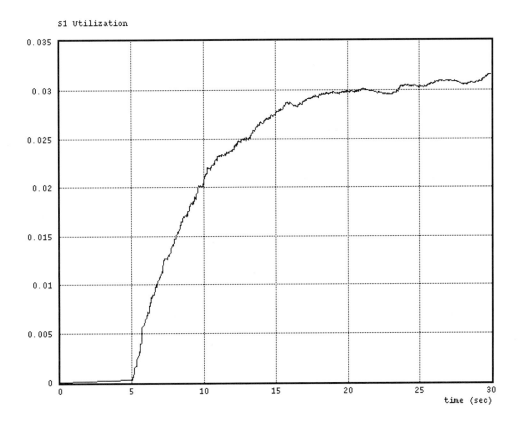

Figure 4.6. S1 Utilization versus Time, Ethernet Protocol.

Note that the **Ethernet Throughput** (bits/sec) statistic measures the average number of bits successfully received by the receiver per unit time. By definition, this statistic counts only the bits associated with collision-free packets.

Answer the following questions:

1. What is the maximum value that the throughput can reach?

2. What is the value of the throughput in steady state?

3. What is the average transmitter utilization in steady state?

4. What is the combined transmitter utilization in steady state?

5. What is the average number of collision counts in S1, in steady state?

6. What is the value of the channel throughput in steady state? (Divide the value you got in question 2 by the channel capacity.)

7. What is the Bus Utilization after **30 sec**?

8. What are the **S1 ETE Delay** and the **ETE Delay**? Compare the two values. What do you observe? Can you give an explanation?

9. What is the Ethernet Total Throughput in steady state?

Total Offered Load

The simulation **application traffic generation rate** input parameter will be varied, in this simulation sequence, to produce different levels of traffic and, hence, different levels of throughput, end-to-end packet delay, and bus utilization. A reasonable level of resolution will be achieved by executing five simulations, each with a different **application traffic generation rate**. Perform the following steps:

1. Modify the simulation sequence by setting the values of the **Application Traffic Generation Rate** attribute to 50, 75, 90, 110, 150.

2. Execute the simulation sequence. OPNET runs the 5 simulations, displaying progress messages as they proceed.

Analysis

The channel throughput and the end-to-end delay as a function of traffic across the simulation sequence will be displayed in the **Analysis Tool**. Each simulation executed by the simulation sequence caused a number of scalar results to be recorded to the Ethernet **output scalar file**.

Plot the **S1 ETE Delay** versus **Total Actual Offered Load**. The resulting graph is given in Figure 4.7.

Using similar steps, plot the **S1 Utilization, S1 Collision Count, Bus Utilization, Ethernet Throughput, Ethernet ETE Delay, Bus Utilization**, and **Bus Throughput** versus **Total Actual Offered Load**.

Answer the following questions:

1. What happens to **S1 Utilization** as the **Total Offered Load** increases? Can you give an explanation?

2. What percentage of the submitted load does the bus carry at low traffic levels?

3. For which load is the maximum throughput achieved?

4. What happens to the **S1 Throughput** and the **Ethernet Throughput** as the offered load increases? Can you give an explanation?

5. What happens to **End-to-End Delay** and **S1 End-to-End Delay** as the offered load increases? Compare the results for the two performance parameters. What do you observe? Can you give an explanation?

6. What happens to **S1 Collision Count** as the **Total Offered Load** increases? Can you give an explanation for the observed results?

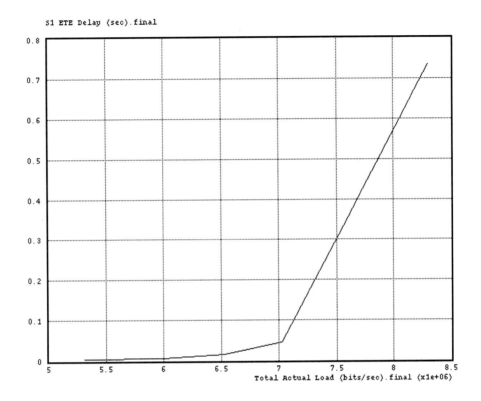

S1 ETE Delay (sec).final

Total Actual Load (bits/sec).final (x1e+06)

Figure 4.7. S1 ETE Delay versus Total Actual Offered Load, Ethernet Protocol.

4.6   Token Ring

A network model has already been created for you and stored in the **token_ring** file. The network models a **Token Ring** system. It consists of a **4 Mbps Token Ring** (TR4 link model) network populated by 8 nodes. The nodes employ the node model **tr_station**.

4.6.1   Specify Probes

A number of statistics will be monitored during simulation. These must be selected using the Probe Editor. A probe file has already been created for you and stored in the **token_ring_probes** file. The following statistics will be monitored:

1. **S1 Actual Load**(bits/sec). Represents the average rate of traffic submitted to the specified token ring layer by the next-higher layer in this node. *Calculation Method:* total bits submitted divided by the current simulation time.

2. **S1 Specified Offered Load**(bits/sec). Represents the calculated load in bits/sec for the specified token ring generator. *Calculation Method:* specified traffic generation rate multiplied by the mean data size.

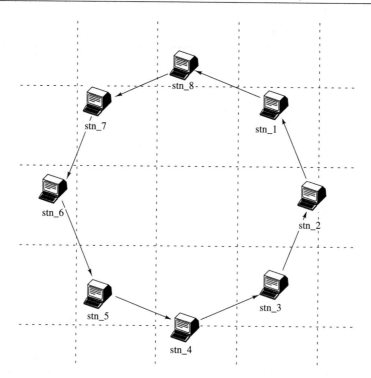

Figure 4.8. Token Ring Network.

3. **S1 Queue Length**(packets). Represents the number of packets stored in the queue.

4. **S1 Thoroughput** (bits/sec). Average bits per second forwarded to the next-higher layer by the specified token ring layer in this node. **Calculation Method**: number of bits forwarded divided by the current simulation time.

5. **S1 Queueing Delay**(sec). Represents instantaneous measurements of packet waiting times in the transmitter's channel's queue.

6. **S1 ETE Delay**(sec). Represents the end-to-end delay of frames accepted by the specified token ring layer in this node. Measured from the time a frame is submitted to the token ring layer of a remote node for transmission to the time the frame is received by this node.

7. **Total Actual Offered Load**(bits/sec). Represents the average rate of traffic submitted to all token link layers in the network by the next-higher layers. *Calculation Method:* total bits submitted divided by the current simulation time.

8. **Total Calculated Offered Load**(bits/sec). Represents the calculated load in bits/sec for all token ring generators in the network. *Calculation Method:* sum of the specified loads for all token ring generators. Specified load is calculated by multiplying specified traffic generation rate by the mean data size.

9. **Token Ring Throughput**(bits/sec). Average bits per second forwarded to the next-higher layers by all token ring layers in the network. *Calculation Method:* number of bits forwarded divided by the current simulation time.

10. **Token Ring ETE Delay**(sec). Represents the end-to-end delay of frames accepted by all token ring layers in the network. Measured from the time a frame is submitted to the token ring layer for transmission to the time the frame is received by the token ring layer of the destination node.

4.6.2 Prepare the Simulation Set Object

A generic simulation set object has been created for you, and stored in the file **token_ring_sim**. Change the parameters of the simulation set object as follows:

1. **Network:** token_ring, **Probe File:** token_ring_probes, **Vector File:** token_ring, **Scalar File:** token_ring.

2. Select as **Seed** any positive number; for example, 11.

3. Set **Duration** to 30, and Update Intvl to 10.

4. Set the **Application Data Size** to 12,000, **Application Start Time** to 5.0, and the **Application Traffic Generation Rate** to 30.

5. Enable the **TR Tx Acceleration** attribute.

Save the simulation sequence in the **token_ring_sim** file.

4.6.3 Simulation Execution and Results Analysis

The goal of the simulation is to observe how the performance of the **Token Ring** protocol varies as a function of the total offered traffic. The performance analysis of the **Token Ring** model will be approached in two different ways. First, we will analyze the performance of the protocol by observing traces of statistics as a function of time for a specific **Total Actual Offered Load** and then we will study the effect of total offered traffic to the **throughput**, **end to end delay**, **queuing delay**, and **queue size** as the total offered load varies.

Trace Analysis at a Specific Total Offered Load

Use the Simulation Tool to execute the simulation sequence that is stored in the **token_ring** simulation set object.

Analysis

1. Use the Analysis Tool to plot the **S1 Throughput**(bits/sec) versus time. The resulting graph is depicted in Figure 4.9.

2. Use similar steps to plot the **S1 Queue Length**, **S1 Queuing Delay**, **S1 ETE Delay**, **Token Ring Throughput**, and **Token Ring ETE Delay** versus time.

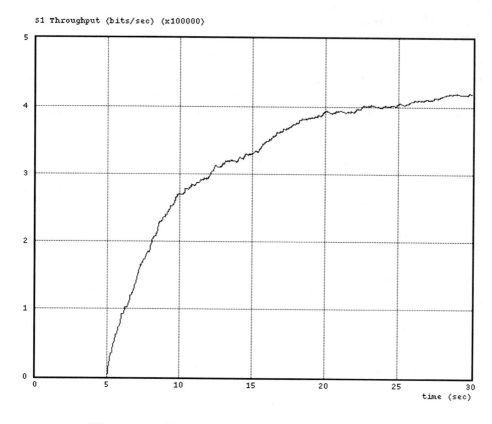

S1 Throughput (bits/sec) (x100000)

time (sec)

Figure 4.9. S1 Throughput versus Time, Token Ring.

Answer the following questions:

1. What is the maximum value that the throughput could reach?

2. What is the value of the throughput in steady state?

3. What is the average transmitter utilization in steady state?

4. What is the combined transmitter utilization in steady state?

5. What is the value of the channel throughput in steady state? (Divide the value you got in question 2 by the channel capacity.)

6. What is the **S1 ETE Delay**?

7. What is the **Token Ring Total Throughput** in steady state?

8. What is the value of mean **Queuing Delay** at S1?

9. What is the value of mean **Queue Length** at S1?

Total Offered Load

The simulation **Application Traffic Generation Rate** input parameter will be varied in this simulation sequence to produce different levels of traffic and, hence, different levels of throughput, end-to-end packet delay, and bus utilization. A reasonable level of resolution will be achieved by executing 4 simulations, each with a different **Application Traffic Generation Rate**. Modify the simulation set object as follows:

1. Set the values of the **Application Traffic Generation Rate** attribute as: 50, 75, 90, 100.

2. Execute the simulation sequence. OPNET runs the 4 simulations, displaying progress messages as they proceed.

Analysis

The channel throughput and the end-to-end delay as a function of traffic across all the simulation sequence will be displayed in the **Analysis Tool**. Each simulation executed by the simulation sequence caused a number of scalar results to be recorded to the **output scalar file**.

1. Open the Analysis Tool.

2. Plot the **S1 Throughput** versus the **Total Offered Load**.

3. Repeat similar steps to also plot the **S1 Queue Length**, **S1 Queuing Delay**, **S1 ETE Delay**, **Token Ring Throughput**, and **Token Ring ETE Delay** versus the **Total Offered Load**.

Answer the following questions:

1. What happens to **S1 Throughput** as **Total Offered Load** increases? Can you give an explanation?

2. What percentage of the submitted load does the bus carry at low traffic levels?

3. For which load is the maximum throughput achieved?

4. What happened to **S1 Throughput** and **Token Ring Throughput** as the offered load increases? Compare the two plots. Can you give an explanation?

5. What happened to **Token Ring ETE Delay** and **S1 ETE Delay** as the offered load increased? Compare the results for the two performance parameters. What do you observe? Can you give an explanation?

6. What happened to **S1 Queuing Delay** and **S1 Queue Length** as the **Total Actual Offered Load** increases? Can you give an explanation for the observed results?

Comparison between Ethernet and Token Ring

In this section we will perform a comparison of the performance between an Ethernet and Token Ring Network under the same load conditions.

1. Use the **ethernet** vector file generated by the experiments of section 4.5.3, and the token_ring vector file generated by the experiments in Section 4.6.3.

2. Plot the **Ethernet Throughput**, and **Ethernet ETE Delay** versus time.

3. Plot the **Token Ring Throughput**, and **Token Ring ETE Delay** versus time.

4. Combine the **Ethernet Throughput** and **Token Ring Throughput** graphs in one plot.

5. Combine the **Ethernet ETE Delay** and **Token Ring ETE Delay** graphs in one plot.

Answer the following questions:

1. What percent of throughput increase does the Token Ring achieve over Ethernet, if any? Explain.

2. What percent of delay decrease, if any, does the Token Ring achieve over Ethernet for the same offered load? Give a justification for your answer.

4.7   Conclusions

1. What is the maximum throughput obtained for each of the four schemes?

2. Rank the four schemes according to the throughput at both low and high loads. How do you explain the ranking?

3. What happened to delay as traffic load increased? What causes this to happen?

4. Rank the four schemes according to delay at both low and high loads. Can you intuitively explain the ranking?

5. Rank the four schemes according to the bus utilization they achieve at both low and high loads.

6. How do the simulation results compare with the theoretical analysis? Can you give some explanations for the discrepancies?

References

[1] Andrew S. Tanenbaum, *Computer Networks*, 3rd Ed., Englewood Cliffs, NJ: Prentice Hall, 1996.

[2] Dimitri Bertsekas and Robert Gallager, *Data Networks*, 2nd Ed., Englewood Cliffs, NJ: Prentice Hall 1987.

[3] Mischa Schwartz, *Telecommunication Networks Protocols, Modeling and Analysis*, Addison-Wesley, 1988.

Chapter 5

Frame Relay

Frame Relay is a connection-oriented (i.e., connection between the communicating parties is set up before the actual data transfer takes place), packet-switching protocol used to pass information across digital interfaces. Other higher-layer protocols are required to handle additional network services, such as flow control and error recovery. The protocol operates at the lower two layers of the *Open Systems Interconnection* (**OSI**) reference model.

Frame Relay is a service for people who want an absolute bare-bones connection-oriented way to move bits from a source to destination at reasonable speed and low cost. Its existence is due to changes in technology over the past few decades. Twenty years ago, communications using telephone lines were slow, analog, and unreliable, while computers were slow and expensive. As a result, complex protocols were required to mask errors, and the users' computers were too expensive to have them do this work [1].

Today, leased telephone lines are fast, digital, and reliable. In addition, computers are fast and inexpensive. Thus, it is possible to use simple transfer protocols, with most of the work of error detection or correction being done by user computers, rather than the network. This is the environment that **Frame Relay** addresses. Frame Relay provides a minimal service, primarily a way to determine the start and end of each frame, and detection of transmission errors. If a bad frame is received, the Frame Relay service simply discards it. It is up to the user to discover that a frame is missing and take the necessary action to recover it.

The network providing a **Frame Relay** interface may be either a carrier-provided public network or a network of privately owned equipment serving a single enterprise. As an interface between user and network equipment, **Frame Relay** provides a method to statistically multiplex many logical channels, referred to as *virtual circuits*, over a single physical transmission line. Assuming that the service is provided between two users, the connection-oriented service requires an agreement between the two end users and the network. The agreement takes place before the data transfer session takes place. Connections and services are premapped. This connection is called a *permanent virtual circuit* or **PVC**.

After a connection has been established, the user data is carried in frames from source to destination. There is no commonly implemented maximum frame size for **Frame Relay**. A network, however, must support at least **262** octets maximum. For **LAN** interconnections a negotiated value of at least **1600** is recommended to prevent the need for *segmentation and reassembly* (**SAR**) of frames by the user equipment.

5.1   Objectives

In this set of simulation experiments, we will study the performance of a Wide Area Network that provides **Frame Relay** services to a number of end users. The objectives of the lab are to:

1. Look at various parameters that characterize the performance of the **Frame Relay** protocol.

2. Access, via simulation, the performance of **Frame Relay** with varying network conditions. Specifically, we will study the **throughput** and **end-to-end delay** performance that the **Frame Relay** provides under different network offered load conditions.

5.2   Preparation

1. What is the difference between connection-oriented and connectionless networks?

2. Describe how a call is established in the case of a connection-oriented network.

3. Describe how a call is established in the case of a connectionless network.

4. Which provides a lower connection establishment delay, a connection-oriented service or a connectionless service? Why?

5. Which provides lower end-to-end delay for data delivery, a connection-oriented service or connectionless service? Why?

6. Which is more reliable, a connection-oriented service or connectionless service?

5.3   Network Model

An example network model has already been created for you and stored in the file **frame_relay_net**. The network models a **Frame Relay** Wide Area Network with generic client server applications that directly utilize **Frame Relay** services. It consists of 4 workstations (**fr4_wkststn** node model) with frame relay capabilities that run FTP type of services, 6 frame relay switching nodes (**fr8_switch**), and one server for initial establishment of connections (**fr4_server** node model). The nodes in the network are connected with point-to-point links (**FR_link** link model). To find out more about the network, use the Network Editor to open the file **frame_relay_net**.

5.4   Specify Probes

A number of statistics will be monitored during simulation. These must be selected using the Probe Editor. A probe file has already been created for you, and is stored in the **frame_relay_probes** file. To learn more about the probe file, use the Probe Editor to open the file **frame_relay_probes**. The following statistics will be monitored during simulation:

1. **FR Actual Load**(bits/sec). Represents the average rate of traffic submitted to all frame relay access devices (FRADs) in the network by the next higher layers. *Calculation Method:* total bits submitted divided by the current simulation time.

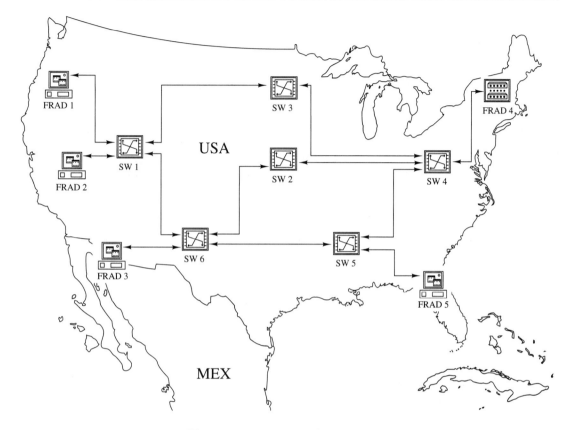

Figure 5.1. Frame Relay Network.

2. **FR Congestion Status**. Congestion detection is based on buffer usage of the various subqueues in the frame relay switch. A statistic value of 0 indicates no congestion; 1 indicates congestion.

3. **FR Residual Error Rate**. Ratio of the total number of frames discarded to total number of frames offered to the network.

4. **Number of Application Active Sessions**. Total number of active sessions in the network.

5. **Number of Server Active Sessions**. Number of active server sessions in the network.

6. **FR Throughput**(bits/sec). Represents the average bits per second forwarded to the next-higher layers by all frame relay access devices (FRADs) in the network. *Calculation Method:* number of bits forwarded divided by the current simulation time.

7. **Server Utilization**. Time-averaged processor utilization for all servers, where 1 indicates that the server is busy and 0 indicates that is idle.

8. **FR ETE Delay**(sec). Represents the end-to-end delay of frames received by all frame relay access devices (FRADs) in the network. Measured from the time a frame is sent from the source node FRAD to the time it is received at the destination node FRAD.

9. **FR ETE Variance**. Represents the variance among end-to-end delays for all frames in the network.

10. **Application Response Time**. Time elapsed between sending a request and receiving the response packet. Measured from the time a client application sends a request to the server to the time it receives a response packet. Every response packet sent for every server to its corresponding destination client application is included in this statistic.

5.5   Prepare the Simulation Set Object

A generic simulation set object has been created for you, and is stored in the file **frame_relay_sim**. To set the parameters of the simulation, use the following steps:

1. Open the Simulation Tool.

2. Read the file **frame_relay_sim** from the menu that pops up.

3. Change the attributes of the simulation set object:

    • **Network:** frame_relay, **Probe File:** frame_relay_probes, **Vector file:** frame_relay, **Scalar file:** frame_relay.

    • Select as **Seed** a positive number, for example, 513.

    • Set **Duration** to 10000, and **Update Intv** to 10.

    • Set **Buffer Capacity** to 512 000. This attribute denotes the buffer capacity (for each subqueue) of the **Frame Relay Switch**, and specifies the maximum number of bits that can be stored in each subqueue in the switch. It is measured in bits.

    • Set **Switching Rate** to 5 000 frames/sec. This attribute denotes the rate at which incoming frames are processed at the switch. It is measured in frames/sec.

4. Save the simulation sequence in the **frame_relay_sim** file.

5.5.1   Simulation Execution and Results Analysis

The goal of the simulation is to observe how the performance of the **Frame Relay** protocol varies as a function of the **offered traffic load** in the network. We will study the effect of **offered traffic load** on **throughput** and **end-to-end delay**. We will also study the effect of **buffer capacity** and **switching rate** on **throughput** and **end-to-end delay**.

5.5.2   Offered Load

The simulation **Client FTP** input parameter will be varied in this simulation sequence to produce different levels of traffic and, hence, different levels of **throughput** and **end-to-end frame delays**. We assume that the network carries FTP traffic only. Modifications can be made to the model to include also other types of traffic. We will examine the performance of the protocol under **low**, **medium**, and **high** levels of **offered traffic**. Several parameters must be entered before the simulation begins.

1. Open the attribute dialog box of the simulation set object **frame_relay** stored in the **frame_relay_sim** simulation sequence file.

2. Define the simulation sequence as follows:

   - Set **Client FTP** to *"low," "medium,"* and *"high"* values.

3. Execute the simulation 3 times, one for each of the load values. Store the simulation traces in different vector files for different offered traffic load levels. In the simulations, the results of the simulation traces will be stored in the vector files **frame_relay1** (for low level of offered traffic), **frame_relay2** (for medium level of offered traffic), and **frame_relay3** (for high level of offered traffic).

Analysis

Residual Error Rate

1. Open the Analysis Tool.

2. Select the **frame_relay2** vector file.

3. Plot the **FR Residual Error Rate** versus Time as in Figure 5.2.

4. Rename the graph to **FR Residual Error Rate** (low load).

5. Repeat the previous two steps for the medium and heavy load (files **frame_relay2** and **frame_relay3** vector files respectively).

6. Name the graphs for the medium and high loads to **FR Residual Error Rate** (medium load), and **FR Residual Error Rate** (high load), respectively.

Answer the following questions:

1. What is the value of the **FR Residual Error Rate** in steady state under **low**, **medium**, and **high** load conditions?

2. What happens to the **FR Residual Error Rate** as the offered traffic increases? Can you explain the observed results?

3. What is the minimum value of the **FR Residual Error Rate**? Under which conditions is it achieved? Explain why.

Frame Relay Throughput

Adapt the steps in the **Residual Error Rate** case to plot the **FR Throughput** under *"low," "medium,"* and *"high"* load conditions.

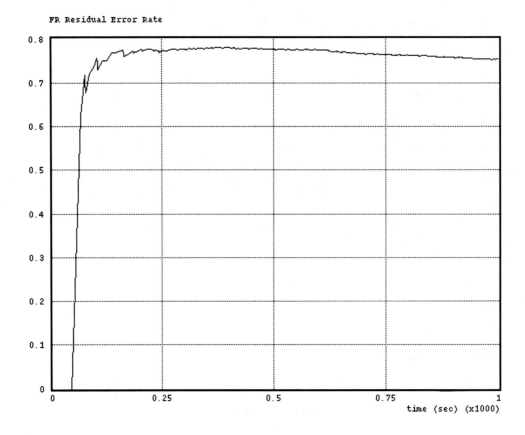

Figure 5.2. FR Residual Error Rate versus Time: Frame Relay Network.

Answer the following questions:

1. What is the value of the **FR Throughput** in steady state under **low, medium**, and **high** load conditions?

2. What percentage of the submitted load does the network carry under **low, medium**, and **high** load conditions?

3. What happens to the **FR Throughput** as the offered traffic increases? Can you explain the observed results?

4. What is the maximum value of the **FR Throughput**? Under which conditions is it achieved? Explain why.

Server Utilization

Adapt the steps in the **Residual Error Rate** case to plot **Server Utilization** under *"low,"* *"medium,"* and *"high"* load conditions.

Answer the following questions:

1. What is the value of the **Server Utilization** in steady state under **low**, **medium**, and **high** load conditions, respectively?

2. What happens to the **Server Utilization** as the offered traffic is increased? Can you explain the observed results?

3. What is the maximum value of the **Server Utilization**? Under which condition is it achieved? Explain why.

FR ETE Delay and FR ETE Variance

Adapt the steps in the **Residual Error Rate** case to plot **FR ETE Delay** and **FR ETE Variance** under *"low,"* *"medium,"* and *"high"* load conditions. Use the Filter model to plot the *time averaged* **FR ETE Delay**, and the *time averaged* **FR ETE Delay Variance** for the three offered load conditions.

Answer the following questions:

1. What is the value of the *time averaged* **FR ETE Delay** and the **FR ETE Variance** in steady state under **low**, **medium**, and **high** load conditions, respectively?

2. What happens to the *time averaged* **FR ETE Delay** and the **FR ETE Variance** as the offered traffic increases? Can you explain why?

3. What is the minimum value of the *time averaged* **FR ETE Delay** in steady state? Under which condition is it achieved? Explain why.

4. Repeat the previous questions for the *time averaged* **FR ETE Delay** and **ETE Delay Variance**. What do you observe?

FR Congestion Status

Adapt the steps in the **Residual Error Rate** case to plot the **FR Congestion Status** under *"low,"* *"medium,"* and *"high"* load conditions.

1. What happens to the **Congestion Status** as the offered traffic is increased? Can you give an intuitive explanation to the observed results?

Active Sessions

Adapt the steps in the **Residual Error Rate** case to plot the **Number of Application Active Sessions** and the **Number of Server Active Sessions** under *"low,"* *"medium,"* and *"high"* load conditions.

Answer the following questions:

1. What is the difference between **Number of Application Active Sessions** and **Number of Server Active Sessions**?

2. What is the value of the **Number of Application Active Sessions** and the **Number of Server Active Sessions** in steady state under **low**, **medium**, and **high** load conditions, respectively?

3. What happens to the **Number of Application Active Sessions** and the **Number of Server Active Sessions** as the offered traffic increases? Can you explain the observed results?

5.5.3   Buffer Capacity

The simulation **Buffer Capacity** input parameter will be varied in this simulation sequence. We will examine the performance of the protocol as the **Buffer Capacity** varies. Define the simulation sequence as follows:

1. Set the values **Client FTP** to *"high."*

2. Select 8 values for the Buffer Capacity in the range 0 to 1,024,000 bits (try to distribute the values uniformly).

3. Deactivate the **Save vector file for each run in set** radio button.

4. Execute the simulation sequence. OPNET displays messages to show the progress of the simulation.

Analysis

1. Open the Analysis Tool.

2. Plot **FR Residual Error Rate** versus **Buffer Capacity**.

3. Plot the rest of the available statistics: **FR Congestion Status**, **FR Throughput**, **Server Utilization**, **ETE Delay**, and **FR ETE Variance**, versus **Buffer Capacity**.

Answer the following questions:

1. What happens to **FR Congestion Status** as the buffer capacity increases? Why?

2. What happens to **FR Residual Error Rate** as the buffer capacity increases? Why?

3. What happens to **FR Throughput** as the buffer capacity increases? Can you give an explanation?

4. What is the effect of buffer capacity on the **Server Utilization**? Can you give an intuitive explanation?

5. What is the effect of buffer capacity on the *time-averaged* **FR ETE Delay** and **FR ETE Variance**? Which of these two statistics does the buffer capacity affect more? Why?

5.5.4   Switching Rate

The simulation **Switching Rate** input parameter will be varied in this simulation sequence. We will examine the performance of the protocol as the **Switching Rate** varies.

Modify the simulation set object as follows:

1. Set the values **Client FTP** to *"high."*

2. Set the **Buffer Capacity** to 512,000 bits.

3. Select 8 values for the **Switching Rate** in the range 1,000–10,000 (try to distribute the values uniformly).

4. Set the **Scalar File** to **frame_relays**.

5. Execute the simulation sequence. OPNET displays messages to show the progress of the simulation.

Analysis

1. Open the Analysis Tool.

2. Plot the **FR Residual Rate** versus **Switching Rate**.

3. Plot the rest of the available statistics: **FR Congestion Status**, **FR Throughput**, **Server Utilization**, **ETE Delay**, and **FR ETE Variance**, versus **Switching Rate**.

Answer the following questions:

1. What happens to **FR Congestion Status** as the switching rate increases? Why?

2. What happens to **FR Residual Error Rate** as the switching rate increases? Why?

3. What happens to **FR Throughput** as the switching rate increases? Can you give an explanation?

4. What is the effect of the switching rate on the **Server Utilization**? Can you give an intuitive explanation?

5. What is the effect of switching rate on the *time-averaged* **FR ETE Delay** and **FR ETE Variance**? Which of these two statistics does the switching rate affect more, and why?

5.6   Conclusions

1. What is the maximum throughput obtained for **Frame Relay**? Under which conditions?

2. What happens to delay and delay variance as the offered load increases? Which parameter is affected more, and why?

3. Of **offered load**, **buffer capacity** and **switching rate**, which has the maximum effect on the **FR Residual Error Rate**, **FR ETE Delay**, **FR ETE Variance**, and **FR Throughput**?

5.7   Extensions

You can repeat the simulation steps and see how the Application Response time varies as the offered load, buffer capacity, and switching rate vary.

References

[1] Andrew S. Tanenbaum, *Computer Networks*, 3rd Ed., Englewood Cliffs, NJ: Prentice Hall, 1996.

Chapter 6

Fiber Distributed Data Interface

The Fiber Distributed Data Interface (**FDDI**) provides general-purpose networking at 100 Mbits/sec transmission rates for a large number of communicating stations configured in a ring or hub topology. Access to the ring bandwidth is controlled through a time token rotation protocol. Each station must receive a token and meet a set of timing and priority criteria before transmitting frames. In order to accommodate network applications in which the response time is critical, FDDI provides for deterministic availability of the ring bandwidth by defining a synchronous transmission service. Asynchronous frame transmission requests dynamically share the remaining ring bandwidth.

A key parameter for FDDI media access protocol is the Target Token Rotation Time (TTRT). The TTRT is a parameter that is, in effect, global to all the stations on the ring, because its value is agreed upon by all stations at ring initialization. The TTRT is the expiration value of the Token Rotation Timer (TRT), which is maintained by each station. This timer holds the time since the token was last captured by a station, and its value defines the permission of the station to transmit frames.

6.1 Objectives

In this set of simulation experiments, we will study the behavior of the FDDI protocol. The objectives of the lab are to:

1. Look at various parameters that characterize the performance of the FDDI protocol.

2. Access, via simulation, the performance of the FDDI protocol. The **throughput**, **delay**, and **link utilization** of an FDDI-based system depends on a number of parameters, such as:

   - Number of stations attached to the ring.
   - Synchronous bandwidth allocation at each station.
   - Requested value of the TTRT by each station (T_Req).
   - The delay incurred by frames and tokens as they traverse a station's ring interface.
   - Propagation delay separating stations on the ring.
   - The mix of asynchronous and synchronous traffic generated at each station.

The task is to observe the performance of the FDDI system as each of the parameters varies.

6.2 Network Model

A network model has already been created for you, and is stored in the **fddi_ring** file. It consists of 8 nodes that transmit and receive information and point-to-point FDDI links. The nodes employ the node model (**fddi_station** node model). The network models an FDDI-based system in a ring topology. To find out more about this network, open the Network Editor and read the **fddi_ring** file.

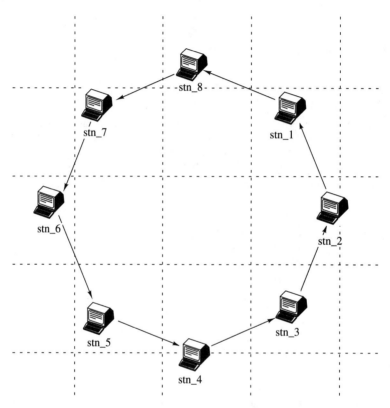

Figure 6.1. FDDI Network.

6.3 Specify Probes

A number of statistics will be monitored during simulation. These must be selected using the Probe Editor. A probe file has already been created for you and stored in the **fddi_ring_probes** file. To find out more about the collected statistics, open the Probe Editor and read the **fddi_ring_probes** file. The following statistics will be monitored during simulation:

1. **S1 Actual Load** (bits/sec). Represents the average rate of traffic submitted to the specified FDDI layer (**S1 node**) by the next-higher layer in this node. *Calculation Method:* total bits submitted divided by the current simulation time.

2. **S1 Actual Load** (packets/sec). Represents the average rate of traffic submitted to the specified FDDI layer (**S1 node**) by the next higher layer in this node. *Calculation Method:* total packets submitted divided by the current simulation time.

3. **S1 ETE Delay** (sec). Represents the end-to-end delay of packets accepted by the specified FDDI layer in this node (**node S1**). Measured from the time a frame is submitted to the FDDI ring of the remote node for transmission to the time the frame is received by this node.

4. **S1 Throughput** (bits/sec). Represents the average bits/sec forwarded to the next-higher layer by the FDDI layer in this node (**node S1**). *Calculation Method:* number of bits forwarded divided by the current simulation time.

5. **S1 Queue Length** (packets). Represents instantaneous measurements of packets waiting in the queue at **node S1**.

6. **S1 Packet Waiting Time** (sec). Represents instantaneous measurements of packet waiting times in the queue at node **S1**.

7. **S1 Throughput** (packets/sec). Represents the average packets/sec forwarded to the next-higher layer by the FDDI layer in this node (**node S1**). *Calculation Method:* number of bits forwarded divided by the current simulation time.

8. **FDDI Actual Load** (bits/sec). Represents the average rate of traffic submitted to all FDDI layers in the network by the next-higher layers. *Calculation Method:* total number of bits submitted divided by the current simulation time.

9. **FDDI Actual Load** (packets/sec). Represents the average rate of traffic submitted to all FDDI layers in the network by the next-higher layers. *Calculation Method:* total number of packets submitted divided by the current simulation time.

10. **FDDI ETE Delay** (sec). Represents the end-to-end delay of packets accepted by all FDDI layers in the network. Measured from the time a packet is submitted to the FDDI layer for transmission to the time the packet is received by the destination node.

11. **FDDI Throughput** (bits/sec). Average bits/sec forwarded to the next-higher layers by all FDDI layers in the network. *Calculation Method:* number of bits forwarded divided by the current simulation time.

6.3.1   Prepare the Simulation Set Object

A generic simulation set object has been created for you and stored in the file **fddi_ring_sim**. Modify the simulation parameters as follows:

1. **Network:** fddi_ring, **Probe file:** fddi_ring_probes, **Vector file:** fddi_ring, **Scalar file:** fddi_ring.

2. Select as **Seed** any positive integer, for example 11.

3. Set **Duration** to 500 and **Update intvl** to 10.

4. Set **FDDI Station Latency** to 1E-07 sec. This attribute denotes the delay incurred by packets as they traverse a station's ring interface.

5. Set **FDDI Hop Propagation Delay** to 3.3E-06 sec. This attribute denotes the time it takes for data to travel from one station to the next.

6. Set **FDDI Sim Acceleration** to 1. This attribute specifies whether the token acceleration mechanism will be employed. A value of 0 indicates that token passing will always be explicitly modeled. The FDDI model incorporates a simulation acceleration feature for modeling the passing of tokens from station to station. When the ring experiences an idle period with no transmissions, the token may be passed many times in a very short period, thus generating many simulation events and consuming large amounts of real time while producing data that are of little interest. In order to jump over these periods, a procedure is employed that blocks the token during idle periods. It is reinjected into the ring as soon as a station again has a need for it.

7. Set **FDDI Spawn Station Offset** to 0. This attribute gives the offset from the lowest station address on the ring. The station with this address will be responsible for creating and inserting a token into the ring.

8. Set **Application Data Size** to 1 024 bits.

9. Set **Application Traffic Generation Rate** to 1.0 packets/sec.

10. Set **FDDI Asynchronous mix** to 50%.

11. Set **FDDI Requested TTRT** to 4.0 sec.

6.4 Simulation Execution and Results Analysis

The goal of the simulation experiments is to observe how the performance of the FDDI ring varies as parameters that affect it vary. The performance analysis of the FDDI Ring model will be approached in two different ways. First, we will analyze the performance of the protocol by observing traces of the monitored statistics for a specific total offered load. Then we will study the effect of the total offered load variation to **throughput**, **delay**, and **utilization** of the system. We will also examine the effect of station latency, hop propagation delay, synchronous/asynchronous mix, and requested TTRT on the performance of the protocol.

6.4.1 Trace Analysis at a Specific Total Offered Load

Execute the Simulation sequence.

Analysis

1. Open the Analysis Tool.

2. Plot **S1 Throughput** versus Time as in Figure 6.2.

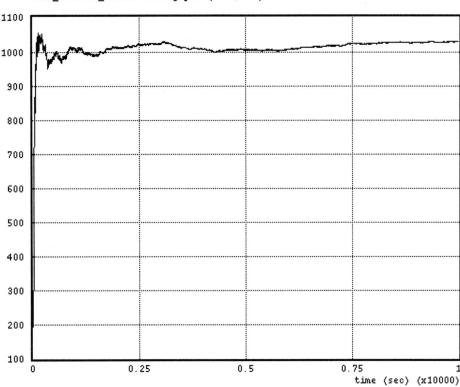

Figure 6.2. S1 Throughput versus Time: FDDI Ring.

3. Use similar steps to plot the rest of the statistics: **S1 Actual Load, S1 ETE Delay, FDDI Total Actual Load, FDDI ETE Delay, FDDI Throughput**, time average **S1 Queue Length**, time average **S1 Queuing Delay**.

Because of the identical interarrival arguments, the ring utilization of the 8 individual transmitters is fairly represented by the one transmitter that is monitored (**S1**).

Answer the following questions:

1. What is the maximum value that the FDDI throughput can reach?

2. What is the value of throughput for **S1** and **FDDI Total Throughput** at steady state? Compare the two values. Give an explanation for the observed results. What is their relationship?

3. What is the average transmitter utilization in steady state?

4. What is the combined transmitter utilization in steady state?

5. What is the value of **S1 ETE Delay** and **FDDI ETE delay** in steady state? Compare the two values. What do you observe? Can you give an explanation?

6. What is the value of time average **Queuing Delay** at S1?

7. What is the value of time average **Queue Length** at S1?

6.4.2   Total Offered Load

In this simulation sequence, the **Application Traffic Generation Rate** input parameter will be varied to produce different levels of traffic and, hence, different levels of throughput, delay and ring utilization. A reasonable level of resolution will be achieved by executing 9 simulations, each with a different **Application Traffic Generation Rate**. Modify the parameters of the simulation set object as in Table 6.1.

Experiment	Simulation Parameters
Effect of Offered Load	Scalar File : fddi_ring_t
	Seed: 11
	Duration: 500
	Update Intvl: 10
	FDDI Station Latency: 10^{-7}
	FDDI Hop Propagation Delay: 3.310^{-6}
	FDDI Sim Acceleration: Enabled
	FDDI Spawn Station Offset: 0
	Application Data Size: 1,024 bits
	Application Traffic Generation Rate:
	1.0, 5.0, 10.0, 20.0, 30.0, 50.0, 70.0, 100.0, 110.0 packets/sec
	FDDI Asynchronous Mix: 50%
	FDDI Requested TTRT : 4.0 sec

Table 6.1. Simulation Parameters for the Offered Load Effect.

Execute the simulation sequence.

Analysis

The throughput and the delay statistics as a function of traffic across all the simulation sequences will be displayed in the **Analysis Tool**. Each simulation executed by the simulation sequence caused a number of scalar results to be recorded to the **output scalar file**.

1. Open the Analysis Tool.

2. Plot **S1 Throughput** versus **Total Offered Load**.

3. Repeat for the rest of the statistics.

Answer the following questions:

1. What happens to the station S1 throughput and the FDDI throughput as the total offered load increases?

2. What percentage of the offered load does the ring carry at low traffic levels? At high traffic levels?

3. For which load is the maximum throughput achieved?

4. What happens to S1 utilization as the total offered load increases? Can you give an explanation?

5. What happens to **S1 ETE Delay** and the **FDDI ETE Delay** as the offered load increases? Compare the results for the two performance parameters. What do you observe? Can you give an explanation?

6. What happens to **S1 Queuing Delay** and the **S1 Queue Length** as the **Total Offered Load** increases? Can you give an explanation for the observed results?

6.4.3   FDDI Station Latency

In this simulation sequence, the **FDDI Station Latency** input parameter is studied to determine its effect on throughput, delay and ring utilization. A reasonable level of resolution will be achieved by executing 8 simulations, each with a different **FDDI Station Latency**. Modify the simulation set object as in Table 6.2.

Analysis

The throughput and the delay statistics as a function of all the simulation sequences will be displayed in the **Analysis Tool**. Each simulation executed by the simulation sequence caused a number of scalar results to be recorded to the output scalar file.

1. Open the Analysis Tool.

2. Plot the **S1 Throughput** versus **FDDI Station Latency**.

3. Repeat for the rest of the statistics.

Answer the following questions:

1. What happens to the station S1 throughput and the FDDI throughput as the **FDDI Station Latency** increases?

2. What percentage of the offered load does the ring carry at low station latency? At high station latency?

Experiment	Simulation Parameters
Effect of FDDI Station Latency	Scalar File : fddi_ring_l Seed: 11 Duration: 500 Update Intvl: 10 FDDI Station Latency: $0 - 10^{-1}$ FDDI Hop Propagation Delay: 3.310^{-6} FDDI Sim Acceleration: Enabled FDDI Spawn Station Offset: 0 Application Data Size: 1 024 bits Application Traffic Generation Rate: 1.0 packets/sec FDDI Asynchronous Mix: 50% FDDI Requested TTRT : 4.0 sec

Table 6.2. Simulation Parameters for the FDDI Station Latency.

3. For which value of station latency is the maximum throughput achieved?

4. What happens to **S1 utilization** as the **FDDI Station Latency** increases? Can you give an explanation?

5. What happens to **S1 ETE Delay** and the **FDDI ETE Delay** as the station latency increases? Compare the results for the two performance parameters. What do you observe? Can you give an explanation?

6. What happens to **S1 Queuing Delay** and the **S1 Queue Length** as the **FDDI Station Latency** increases? Can you give an explanation for the observed results?

6.4.4   FDDI Hop Propagation Delay

In this simulation sequence, the **FDDI Hop Propagation Delay** input parameter is studied to determine its effect on throughput, delay, and ring utilization. A reasonable level of resolution will be achieved by executing 8 simulations, each with a different **FDDI Hop Propagation Delay**. Modify the simulation set object as in Table 6.3.

Analysis

The throughput and the delay statistics as a function of all the simulation sequences will be displayed in the **Analysis Tool**. Each simulation executed by the simulation sequence caused a number of scalar results to be recorded to the **output scalar file**.

1. Plot the **S1 ETE Delay** versus the **FDDI Hop Propagation Delay**.

2. Similarly plot the rest of the statistics.

Experiment	Simulation Parameters
Effect, FDDI Hop Propagation Delay	Scalar File : fddi_ring_1 Seed: 11 Duration: 500 Update Intvl: 10 FDDI Station Latency: 10^{-7} FDDI Hop Propagation Delay: $0\text{-}3.310^{-6}$ FDDI Sim Acceleration: Enabled FDDI Spawn Station Offset: 0 Application Data Size: 1 024 bits Application Traffic Generation Rate: 1.0 packets/sec FDDI Asynchronous Mix: 50% FDDI Requested TTRT : 4.0 sec

Table 6.3. Simulation Parameters for the FDDI Hop Propagation Delay.

Answer the following:

1. What happens to the station **S1 throughput** and the **FDDI throughput** as the **FDDI Hop Propagation Delay** increases?

2. What percentage of the offered load does the ring carry at low propagation delay? At high propagation delay?

3. For which value of **FDDI Hop Propagation Delay** is the maximum throughput achieved?

4. What happens to **S1 utilization** as **FDDI Hop Propagation Delay** increases? Can you give an explanation?

5. What happens to **S1 ETE Delay** and **FDDI ETE Delay** as **FDDI Hop Propagation Delay** increases? Compare the results for the two performance parameters. What do you observe? Can you give an explanation?

6. What happens to **S1 Queuing Delay** and **S1 Queue Length** as **FDDI Hop Propagation Delay** increases? Can you give an explanation for the observed results?

6.4.5   FDDI Asynchronous Mix

In this simulation sequence, the **FDDI Asynchronous Mix** input parameter is studied to determine the effect on throughput, delay, and ring utilization. A reasonable level of resolution will be achieved by executing 8 simulations, each with a different **FDDI Asynchronous Mix**. Modify the simulation set object as in Table 6.4:

Experiment	Simulation Parameters
Effect of FDDI Asynchronous Mix	Scalar File : fddi_ring_a Seed: 11 Duration: 500 Update Intvl: 10 FDDI Station Latency: 10^{-7} FDDI Hop Propagation Delay: 3.310^{-6} FDDI Sim Acceleration: Enabled FDDI Spawn Station Offset: 0 Application Data Size: 1 024 bits Application Traffic Generation Rate: 1.0 packets/sec FDDI Asynchronous Mix: 0–100% FDDI Requested TTRT : 4.0 sec

Table 6.4. Simulation Parameters for the FDDI Asynchronous Mix.

Analysis

The throughput and the delay statistics as a function of all the simulation sequences will be displayed in the **Analysis Tool**. Each simulation executed by the simulation sequence caused a number of scalar results to be recorded to the output scalar file.

1. Open the Analysis Tool.

2. Plot the **S1 Queuing Delay** versus **FDDI Asynchronous Mix**.

3. Similarly plot the rest of the statistics.

Answer the following questions:

1. What happens to the station **S1 throughput** and the **FDDI throughput** as the **FDDI Asynchronous Mix** increases?

2. For which value of **FDDI Asynchronous Mix** is the maximum throughput achieved?

3. What happens to **S1 utilization** as **FDDI Asynchronous Mix** increases? Can you give an explanation?

4. What happens to **S1 ETE Delay** and **FDDI ETE Delay** as **FDDI Asynchronous Mix** increases? Compare the results for the two performance parameters. What do you observe? Can you give an explanation?

5. What happens to **S1 Queuing Delay** and **S1 Queue Length** as the **FDDI Asynchronous Mix** increases? Can you give an explanation for the observed results?

6.4.6   FDDI Requested TTRT

In this simulation sequence, the **FDDI Requested TTRT** input parameter is to be studied to determine its effect on throughput, delay, and ring utilization. A reasonable level of resolution will be achieved by executing 8 simulations, each with a different **FDDI Requested TTRT**. Modify the simulation set object as in Table 6.5:

Experiment	Simulation Parameters
Effect of FDDI Asynchronous Mix	Scalar File : fddi_ring_r
	Seed: 11
	Duration: 500
	Update Intvl: 10
	FDDI Station Latency: 10^{-7}
	FDDI Hop Propagation Delay: $3.3\dot{1}0^{-6}$
	FDDI Sim Acceleration: Enabled
	FDDI Spawn Station Offset: 0
	Application Data Size: 1 024 bits
	Application Traffic Generation Rate: 1.0 packets/sec
	FDDI Asynchronous Mix: 50%
	FDDI Requested TTRT: 0–10.0 sec

Table 6.5. Simulation Parameters for the FDDI Requested TTRT.

Analysis

The throughput and the delay statistics as a function of all the simulation sequences will be displayed in the **Analysis Tool**. Each simulation executed by the simulation sequence caused a number of scalar results to be recorded to the output scalar file.

1. Open the Analysis Tool.

2. Plot the **S1 Queue Length** versus **FDDI Requested TTRT**.

3. Similarly plot the rest of the statistics.

Answer the following questions:

1. What happens to the station **S1 throughput** and the **FDDI throughput** as the **FDDI Requested TTRT** increases?

2. For which value of the **FDDI Requested TTRT** is the maximum throughput achieved?

3. What happens to **S1 utilization** as **FDDI Requested TTRT** increases? Can you give an explanation?

4. What happens to **S1 ETE Delay** and **FDDI ETE Delay** as the **FDDI Requested TTRT** increases? Compare the results for the two performance parameters. What do you observe? Can you give an explanation?

5. What happens to **S1 Queuing Delay** and the **S1 Queue Length** as the **FDDI Requested TTRT** increases? Can you give an explanation for the observed results?

6.5   Conclusions

1. What is the maximum throughput obtained by the FDDI ring?

2. What happens to delay as the traffic load increases?

3. Rank the following parameters by the effect they have on total throughput: **FDDI Hop Propagation Delay, FDDI Station Latency, T_Req, Asynchronous/Synchronous Mix, Application Traffic Generation Rate**. Can you give an intuitive justification for the ranking?

4. Rank the following parameters as to the effect they have on the FDDI ETE Delay: **FDDI Hop Propagation Delay, FDDI Station Latency, T_Req, Asynchronous/ Synchronous Mix, Application Traffic Generation Rate**. Can you give an intuitive justification for the ranking?

5. Rank the following parameters by the effect they have on the total queuing delay: **FDDI Hop Propagation Delay, FDDI Station Latency, T_Req, Asynchronous/ Synchronous Mix, Application Traffic Generation Rate**. Can you give an intuitive justification for the ranking?

6. Rank Ethernet, Token Ring, and FDDI ring by throughput, utilization, and delay. Can you intuitively explain the ranking? Note that, for this part, you need some of the results from Chapter 4.

Chapter 7

Job Service Disciplines

The *Job Service Discipline* set of models addresses the issue of managing limited access to a single resource. The resource being modeled can be a single multiprocessor CPU, a disk drive, a communications channel, a computer bus, or a page of memory.

Objects that wish to access the resource send requests, or *jobs*, to the resource manager. Because the resource is often unable to give immediate service to all jobs, queuing is required. The resource can manage requests for access according to different schemes, or disciplines. These disciplines may be designed to achieve certain performance goals, such as:

- Provide greater resource access for prioritized requests.

- Maximize overall throughput (minimize average delay).

- Provide fairness (minimize variation in delay).

- Maximize the number of requests in the system (size of the queue).

The model scope is limited to the behavior of the resource itself. The resource receives requests for access and manages its own service for those requests. No constraints are placed on the entities issuing the job requests. From the point of view of the requesting entity, the resource interface requires it, first of all, to send a request and represent a job, and then to receive a reply that the job has completed service. The requestor may block other activities between the request and reply, or instead may continue to perform other actions. The model implementation assumes that there is no overhead processing time required to change the job in service.

7.1   First-In First-Out Service Job Discipline

7.1.1   Network Model

An example network model has already been created for you, and is stored in the file **jsd_fifo**. The network models a FIFO discipline server. Incoming packets are enqueued at the tail of the queue, and service times are completed in one consecutive block. Enqueued packets wait for the completion of service of earlier-arriving packets before they begin service. Thus, the queue behaves in the *First-In First-Out* (**FIFO**) manner. To find out more about the network, use the Network Editor to open the file **jsd_fifo**. A FIFO system is generally depicted as in Figure 7.1.

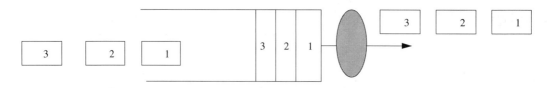

Figure 7.1. FIFO Queue.

7.1.2   Specify Probes

A number of statistics will be monitored during simulation. These were selected using the Probe Editor. A probe file has already been created for you, and is stored in the **jsd_fifo** file. The following statistics are monitored during simulation:

1. **Jsd Busy Status**. Represents server utilization. One (1) indicates that the server is busy; 0, that it is idle.

2. **Jsd Delay**. Represents the delay experienced by a completing job over and above its service time when the job leaves the queue. *Calculation Method:* queue departure time minus the sum of queue entrance and service time.

3. **Jsd Remaining Work**. Instantaneous work left in the queue. Each time a job enters or leaves the queue, this statistic records the total of all service times remaining for all packets still in the queue.

4. **Jsd Normalized Delay**. *Calculation Method:* total time a job spends in the queue divided by service time. A job that experiences no delay in the queue beyond its required service time has a normalized delay of 1.0.

5. **Jsd Windowed Utilization**. Time-averaged server utilization during the most recent time window, when 1 indicates that the server is busy, and 0, that it is idle.

6. **Jsd Average Remaining Work** (sec). Represents the average amount of work remaining in the queue during each time window.

7. **Jsd Queue Length**. Represents the number of packets stored in the queue.

8. **Mean Utilization**. Represents an overall measure of server utilization. *Calculation Method:* total busy time of the server divided by the current simulation time.

9. **Average Throughput.** Represents the average work completed per time unit. *Calculation Method:* total work completed by the queue divided by the current simulation time.

10. **Mean Processing Delay** (sec). Represents the average delay experienced by all jobs. *Calculation Method:* total processing delay divided by the number of jobs serviced.

7.1.3   Prepare the Simulation Set Object

A generic simulator set object has been created for you, and is stored in the file **jsd_fifo**. Modify the attributes of the simulation set object as follows. The resulting simulation set object is shown in Figure 7.2.

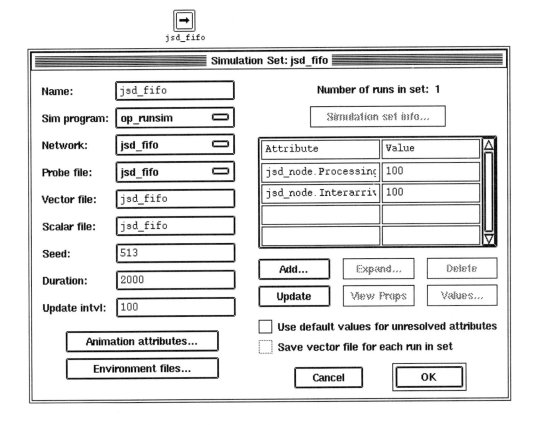

Figure 7.2. Simulation Set Object: FIFO Queue.

1. **Network:** jsd_fifo, **Probe file:** jsd_fifo, **Vector file:** jsd_fifo, **Scalar File:** jsd_fifo.

2. Select as **Seed** a positive number; for example, 513.

3. Set **Duration** to 2000, and **Update intvl** to 100.

4. Set **Interarrival Time** to 100, and **Processing Rate** to 100.

Save the simulation sequence in the **jsd_fifo** file.

7.1.4   Simulation Execution and Results Analysis

The goal of the simulation is to observe how the performance of the FIFO discipline system varies as a function of the offered load and the processing rate of the server.

Offered Load

   The simulation **Interarrival Times** input parameter will be varied in this simulation sequence to produce different levels of traffic and, hence, different levels of throughput, delays, and number of jobs in the queue. First, modify the simulation set object's attributes as in Table 7.1. Then, run the simulation sequence.

Analysis

1. Open the Analysis Tool.

2. Plot **Jsd Delay** versus **Interarrival Times**. The resulting graph is given in Figure 7.3.

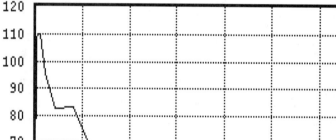

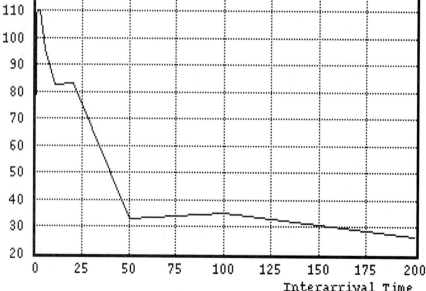

Figure 7.3. Jsd Delay versus Interarrival Times: FIFO Queue.

3. Repeat similar steps to plot the rest of the monitored statistics.

Experiment	Simulation Parameters
Effect of Offered Load	Scalar File : jsd_fifo Seed: 513 Duration: 20000 Update Intvl: 100 Interarrival Times: 0.1, 0.2, 0.5, 1, 2, 5, 20, 30, 50, 100, 200 Processing Rate: 100

Table 7.1. Simulation Parameters for the Offered Load Effect.

Answer the following questions:

1. What happens to the **Jsd Busy Status** as the offered load increases (Interarrival Time decreases)?

2. What happens to the **Jsd Delay** as the offered load increases (Interarrival Time decreases)?

3. What happens to the **Jsd Remaining Work** as the offered load increases (Interarrival Time decreases)?

4. What happens to the **Jsd Normalized Delay** as the offered load increases (Interarrival Time decreases)?

5. What happens to the **Jsd Average Remaining Work** as the offered load increases (Interarrival Time decreases)?

6. What happens to the **Jsd Queue Length** as the offered load increases (Interarrival Time decreases)?

7. What happens to the **Jsd Mean Utilization** as the offered load increases (Interarrival Time decreases)?

8. What happens to the **Jsd Average Throughput** as the offered load increases (Interarrival Time decreases)?

9. What happens to the **Jsd Mean Processing Delay** as the offered load increases (Interarrival Time decreases)?

Processing Rate

The simulation **Processing Rate** input parameter will be varied in this simulation sequence to produce different levels of service rates and, hence, different levels of throughput, delay, and number of jobs in the queue. First, modify the simulation set object as in Table 7.2. Then excecute the simulation sequence.

Experiment	Simulation Parameters
Effect of Processing Rate	Scalar File : jsd_fifo1 Seed: 513 Duration: 20000 Update Intvl: 100 Interarrival Time: 100 Processing Rate: 50–10,000

Table 7.2. Simulation Parameters for the Processing Rate Effect.

1. Plot the same statistics as in the **Interarrival Times** experiments.

2. Answer the same set of questions as in the **Interarrival Times** analysis.

7.2   Priority Job Service Discipline

7.2.1   Network Model

An example network model has already been created for you, and is stored in the file **jsd_prio**. The network models a priority job service discipline. Incoming packets are enqueued according to their priority. Higher-priority packets are enqueued toward the head of the queue, while lower priority packets are enqueued toward the tail. Priority is determined on the basis of the packet's predefined **priority** field, which can be set beforehand. Once a packet begins service, it remains in uninterrupted service at the head of the queue until it completes service, regardless of any other packet arrival with higher priority. To find out more about the network, use the Network Editor to open the file **jsd_prio**. The node level of the priority job service discipline network is given in Figure 7.4.

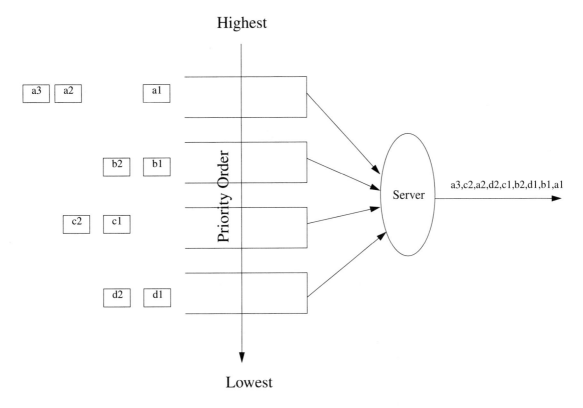

Figure 7.4. Priority Job Service Discipline Network.

7.2.2   Specify Probes

A number of statistics will be monitored during simulation. These must be selected using the Probe Editor. A probe file has already been created for you, and is stored in the **jsd_prio** file. The same statistics as in the **jsd_fifo** are monitored.

7.2.3   Prepare the Simulation Set Object

A generic simulator set object has been created for you, and is stored in the file **jsd_prio**. Modify the simulation set object's attributes as in Figure 7.5.

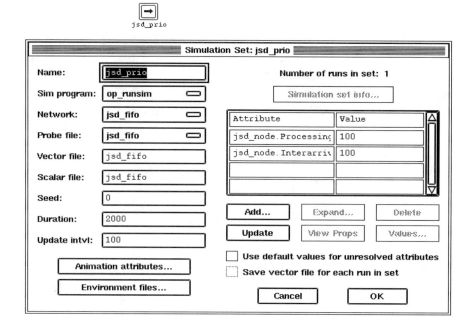

Figure 7.5. Simulation Set Object: JSD Queue.

7.2.4   Simulation Execution and Results Analysis

The goal of the simulation is to observe how the performance of the FIFO discipline system varies as a function of the offered load, and the processing rate of the server.

Offered Load

Follow the same steps as in the **jsd_fifo** case. Answer the same set of analysis questions.

Interarrival Times

Follow the same steps as in the **jsd_fifo** case. Answer the same set of analysis questions.

7.3   Preempt and Resume Job Service Discipline

7.3.1   Network Model

An example network model has already been created for you and stored in the file **jsd_prmpt_res**. The network models a preempt and resume job service discipline. As in the **jsd_prio** case, incoming packets are enqueued according to the value of their priority fields. However, if a packet with higher priority arrives while a packet is in service, the packet in service is preempted. Its service time is interrupted, and the packet is rescheduled within the queue. Its remaining service time is updated to reflect the service already completed. Meanwhile, the newly arrived higher-priority packet will enter service. To find out more about the network, use the Network Editor to open the file **jsd_prmpt_res**.

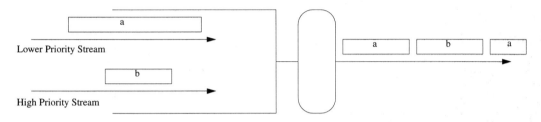

Figure 7.6. Preempt and Resume Job Service Discipline Queue.

7.3.2   Specify Probes

A number of statistics will be monitored during simulation. These must be selected using the Probe Editor. A probe file has already been created for you, and is stored in the **jsd_prmpt_res** file. The same statistics as in the **jsd_fifo** are monitored.

7.3.3   Prepare the Simulation Set Object

7.3.4   Simulation Execution and Results Analysis

The goal of the simulation is to observe how the performance of the preempt and resume job service discipline system varies as a function of the offered load and the processing rate of the server.

Offered Load

Follow the same steps as in the **jsd_fifo** case. Answer the same set of analysis questions.

Interarrival Times

Follow the same steps as in the **jsd_fifo** case. Answer the same set of analysis questions.

7.4   Processor Sharing

7.4.1   Network Model

An example network model has already been created for you, and is stored in the file **jsd_proc_share**. The network models a processor-sharing job service discipline. Packets are serviced concurrently in this discipline. Each packet is serviced at a rate that is the processing rate of the queue divided by the number of packets in the queue. Thus, the queue shares its processing resources evenly among all of the packets in the queue at any given time. To find out more about the network, use the Network Editor to open the file **jsd_proc_share**.

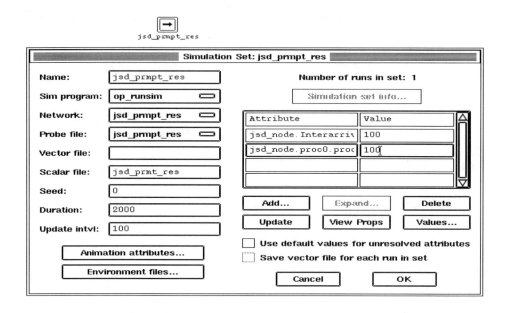

Figure 7.7. Simulation Set Object: Preempt and Resume Job Service Discipline Queue.

7.4.2 Specify Probes

A number of statistics will be monitored during simulation. These must be selected using the Probe Editor. A probe file has already been created for you and stored in the **jsd_proc_share** file. The same statistics as in the **jsd_fifo** are monitored.

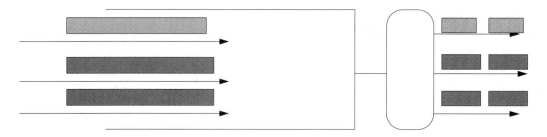

Figure 7.8. Processor Sharing.

7.4.3   Prepare the Simulation Set Object

A generic simulation set object has been created for you, and is stored in the file **jsd_proc_share**. Modify the attributes of the simulation as in Figure 7.9.

7.4.4   Simulation Execution and Results Analysis

The goal of the simulation is to observe how the performance of the processor sharing job service discipline system varies as a function of the offered load, and the processing rate of the server.

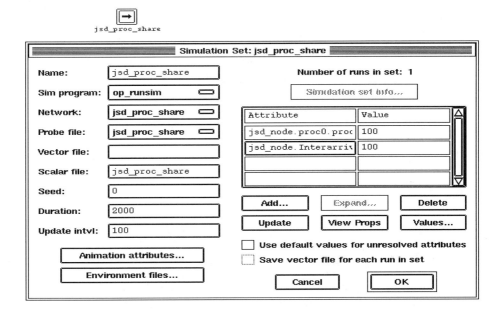

Figure 7.9. Simulation Set Object: Processor Sharing.

Offered Load

Follow the same steps as in the **jsd_fifo** case. Answer the same set of analysis questions.

Interarrival Times

Follow the same steps as in the **jsd_fifo** case. Answer the same set of analysis questions.

7.5   Shortest First Job Service Discipline

7.5.1   Network Model

An example network model has already been created for you and stored in the file **jsd_sjf**. The network models a Shortest Job First Service Discipline. Incoming packets are enqueued in the priority order so that shorter jobs are enqueued at the head of the queue, and longer jobs toward the tail. This discipline behaves similarly to **jsd_prio**, except that the priority of packets is based on their service times rather than on the value of their priority fields. As in the **jsd_prio**, once a packet has entered service, it cannot be interrupted by the arrival of other jobs. To find out more about the network, use the network editor to open the file **jsd_sjf**.

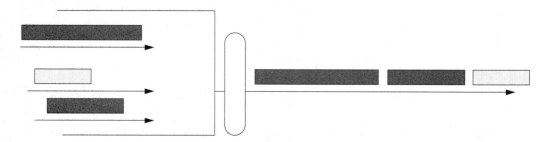

Figure 7.10. Shortest First Job Service Discipline.

7.5.2   Specify Probes

A number of statistics will be monitored during simulation. These must be selected using the Probe Editor. A probe file has already been created for you, and is stored in the **jsd_sjf** file. The same statistics as in the **jsd_fifo** are monitored.

7.5.3   Prepare the Simulation Set Object

A generic simulation set object has been created for you, and is stored in the file **jsd_sjf**. Modify the attributes of the simulation as in Figure 7.11.

7.5.4   Simulation Execution and Results Analysis

The goal of the simulation is to observe how the performance of the Shortest First Job Service Discipline system varies as a function of the offered load and the processing rate of the server.
Offered Load
    Follow the same steps as in the **jsd_fifo** case. Answer the same set of analysis questions.

Interarrival Times
    Follow the same steps as in the **jsd_fifo** case. Answer the same set of analysis questions.

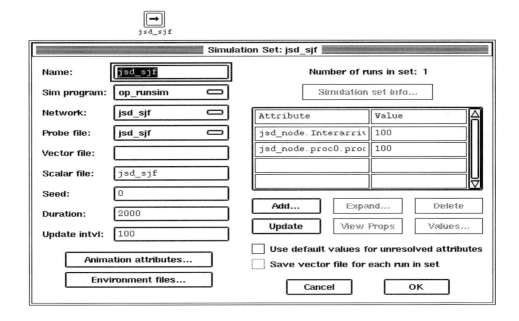

Figure 7.11. Simulation Set Object: Shortest First Job Service Discipline.

7.6 Conclusions

1. Rank the service disciplines according to their ability to give resource access to prioritized requests.

2. Rank the disciplines according to the throughput they provide for the same conditions. Which job discipline provides the maximum throughput under the same conditions? Which job discipline provides the minimum? Can you give an intuitive explanation?

3. Rank the job disciplines according to decreasing average delay. Can you give an intuitive explanation?

4. Rank the job disciplines according to the fairness they provide to the requests. Which discipline is the most fair? Which is the least?

5. Rank the job disciplines according to decreasing variation in delay. Can you explain intuitively the observed results?

6. Rank the disciplines according to decreasing average number of requests in the system. What do you observe? Can you give an explanation?

Accessing the Lab Models

The CD-ROM accompanying *Modeling and Simulating Communication Networks* contains model and support files for each lab. To use the models with the labs, you must first make them available to OPNET as follows:

1. Make certain that OPNET has been installed and at least one user account has been created.

2. Copy the directory for each lab you want to perform from the **/models** directory on the CD-ROM to your workstation's hard drive. Any location in the file system is acceptable, but a convenient location in the OPNET directory structure is
   <mil3_directory>/*<release_directory>*/**models**.

3. Add the lab directories to the environment database of each user account that needs to access the lab models:

   a. Open the environment database file (*<HOME>*/**op_admin/env_db***<release>*) in any text editor.

   b. Add the path name of each lab directory to the list of model directories following the **mod_dirs** attribute. For example, after adding the model directory for the M/M/1 lab in chapter 2, the directory list should resemble this:

   > •
   >
   > •
   >
   > mod_dirs :   /user/dtaylor/op_models,
   >   /user/mil3/4.0.A/models/ch2_mm1,
   >   /user/mil3/4.0.A/models/std/anim_samp,
   >
   > •
   >
   > •

   c. Save the environment database file.